KARATE'S
MODERN
MASTERS

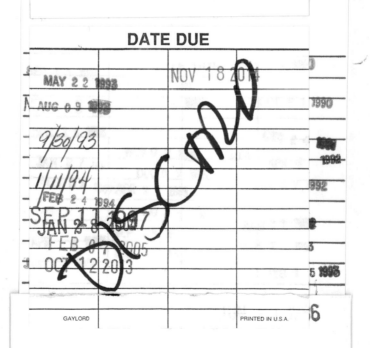

KARATE'S
MODERN MASTERS

THE PHILOSOPHIES AND TECHNIQUES
OF THE ART'S
LIVING LEGENDS

THE EDITORS OF
OFFICIAL KARATE MAGAZINE
WITH GEORGE R. PARULSKI, JR.

CONTEMPORARY
BOOKS, INC.
CHICAGO

Library of Congress Cataloging in Publication Data

Main entry under title:
  Karate's modern masters.

  Includes index.
  1. Karate.   2. Karate—History.   3. Martial artists.
I. Parulski, George R.   II. Official Karate.
GV1114.3.K39   1985   796.8'153   85-17476
ISBN 0-8092-5309-7

Published by Contemporary Books, Inc.
180 North Michigan Avenue, Chicago, Illinois 60601
Manufactured in the United States of America
Library of Congress Catalog Card Number: 85–17476
International Standard Book Number: 0-8092-5309-7

Published simultaneously in Canada by Beaverbooks, Ltd.
195 Allstate Parkway, Valleywood Business Park
Markham, Ontario L3R 4T8 Canada

This is for you, Jackie,
with all my love

TABLE OF CONTENTS

ACKNOWLEDGMENTS   ix

FOREWORD   x

INTRODUCTION   xii

A NOTE ON USING THIS BOOK   xiv

P A R T I: HISTORY   1

CHAPTER 1
THE HISTORY OF TRADITIONAL KARATE   3

CHAPTER 2
KARATE IN AMERICA   7

P A R T II: KATA   17

CHAPTER 3
FRANKIE "DR. SPEED" MITCHELL   19
GOJUSHI-HO KATA OF SHORIN-RYU

CHAPTER 4
GEORGE R. PARULSKI, JR.   31
KANKU-DAI OF SHOTOKAN KARATE WITH TIPS ON WINNING KATA COMPETITION

CHAPTER 5
PETER MANFREDI   47
KANKU-SHO OF SHOTOKAN KARATE

CHAPTER 6
FRANK VAN LENTEN   58
THE HIDDEN HANDS (HIMITSU) OF KATA

P A R T III: FREE-FIGHTING   67

CHAPTER 7
CHUCK NORRIS   69
BUILDING EFFECTIVE COMBINATIONS

CHAPTER 8
BILL "SUPERFOOT" WALLACE   75
USING THE LEGS EFFECTIVELY

CHAPTER 9
PETER MUSACCHIO   80
EFFECTIVE GOJU-RYU KARATE COMBINATIONS

CHAPTER 10
JOE LEWIS   87
EFFECTIVE HAND TECHNIQUES FOR POINT COMPETITION

CHAPTER 11
MARK McCARTHY   91
THE DOUBLE KICK

CHAPTER 12
RANDY PUMPUTIS   94
ISSHIN-RYU KARATE SPORT COMBINATIONS

CHAPTER 13
ED FOX   100
EFFECTIVE COMBINATIONS USING KUNG-FU AND KARATE

CHAPTER 14
SUK JUN KIM   106
ADVANCED TAEKWON-DO COMBINATIONS

CHAPTER 15
MICHELLE MAZZOCHETTI   109
A WOMAN'S VIEW OF FREE-FIGHTING

CHAPTER 16
DOUG IVAN   114
THROWING THE PERFECT KICK

CHAPTER 17
JEAN DUTEAU   118
CLASSICAL CHINESE FREE-FIGHTING COMBINATIONS

CHAPTER 18
DAN IVAN   124
FAVORITE FREE-FIGHTING TECHNIQUES

PART IV: SELF-DEFENSE   129

CHAPTER 19
KICHIRO SHIMABUKU   130
TRADITIONAL ISSHIN-RYU KARATE AS SELF-DEFENSE

CHAPTER 20
MAS OYAMA   136
KYOKUSHINKAI-KAN KARATE AGAINST A GUN

CHAPTER 21
DEBRA MAZZOCHETTI   139
SELF-DEFENSE FOR WOMEN

CHAPTER 22
FUMIO DEMURA   143
SHITO-RYU KARATE AS SELF-DEFENSE

CHAPTER 23
PETER MANFREDI   146
MIXING BOXING AND KARATE FOR SELF-DEFENSE

CHAPTER 24
FRANKIE "DR. SPEED" MITCHELL   150
SELF-DEFENSE IN SPECIAL SITUATIONS

CHAPTER 25
GEORGE R. PARULSKI, JR.   155
MIXING KARATE AND JUJUTSU

PART V: WEAPONS   161

CHAPTER 26
RICHARD BROOKS   163
ANCIENT OKINAWAN WEAPONS

CHAPTER 27
RON DUNCAN   168
MODERN-DAY NINJA DEMONSTRATES USE OF SHORT STICK

INDEX   173

ACKNOWLEDGMENTS

The author wishes to express his sincere thanks to the following people: (1) to Al Weiss, editor at *Official Karate* magazine for his coauthorship of this book and his support of this project; (2) to Alan Paul, managing editor at *Official Karate*, and David Weiss, editor at *Warriors* magazine, for helping gather photos and information to make this book possible; (3) to Carolyn Parulski, for photographing the sequences in Chapters 4, 23, and 25; (4) and to the many photographers who granted *Official Karate* the permission to use the black-and-white photos that appear in this book.

FOREWORD

In my many years sitting at the editor's desk at *Official Karate* magazine, I have had the opportunity to watch American karate evolve from an idea to a living, breathing entity—and I hope *Official Karate* played a significant part in this growth.

I first met author George R. Parulski, Jr., when he sent us a story in 1976 called "The Art of Japanese Swordsmanship." It was the first of some 70 articles written by him for *Official Karate* and its sister publications.

When he approached me about cowriting and endorsing this project I thought to myself "Not another karate book! There are so many on the market already. How can this one be different?" I changed my tune when I saw the material and the format he intended to use. Just think: a karate book that highlights the specialty techniques of American karate's superstars, the up-and-coming masters. Indeed here is a karate book like no other.

The value of such a text lies not in its pretty pictures, but in the meaning behind those pictures. Each chapter can be looked at as a seminar. And looking over the table of contents, you will see that you will be getting seminars from the very best. By studying the photos and explanations carefully, you will see how the masters punch, how they kick, how they shift their body weight. These are the subtleties that make these superstars masters in their own right. And by carefully studying these photos, you too can learn their secrets.

The greatest secret, so to speak, of the superstars is not so much technique but rather conditioning and determination. Hard work and constant practice is what makes superstars of us all.

To accomplish his goal, Parulski has divided the book into five parts, each highlighting a particular part of karate: history, kata, self-defense, free-fighting, and weapons.

The history section looks at karate in its traditional light as well as in America. Parulski has taken the time to research this material, and his efforts have produced a clear, clean, accurate history of karate as it practiced today.

The section on kata presents the classical formal exercises of karate. Parulski has selected three kata: *kanku-dai, kanku-sho, and goju-*

shi-ho. The kanku kata have been selected because they are perhaps the oldest kata in existence today, developed by Gichin Funakoshi from the orginal Okinawan *kusanku* form. Gojushi-ho was selected because it is representative of the variety found in Okinawan karate.

The section on self-defense presents many mixtures of martial arts. Demonstrated is karate mixing with boxing and jujutsu as well as classical karate and a woman's point of view.

The section on free-fighting will be of special interest to today's practicing karateka. Presented here are the movements of the very best in the field—Chuck Norris and Bill "Superfoot" Wallace, to name a few.

No karate book would be complete without at least a mention of weapons. Therefore, the last section in this book deals with weapons. This section outlines traditional usage as well as modern-day self-defense with the short staff.

It is my sincere feeling that the text you hold in your hands is the most unusual karate manual of its kind. No other book comes close to the concept on which *Karate's Modern Masters* is based: to show—through brotherhood of styles and practitioners—the specialties of karate leaders and teachers.

Al Weiss
Editor, *Official Karate* magazine
Publisher, *Warriors* magazine
Publisher, *American Karate* magazine

PREFACE

The world of karate is unique because within its realm there is something for everyone. For those seeking physical fitness, self-discipline, self-defense, philosophical guidance, or even a challenging game, karate has something to offer.

It is because of its multifaceted nature that karate has found a home in America. As Americans, we love to pull things apart and make them adapt to us and our way of thinking. Karate has stood the test of time and has become another American institution—right along with Mom's apple pie.

As karate has grown to teach the hearts of many Americans, we, as a nation, have produced our own brand of superstars. Names like Chuck Norris and Bill Wallace are familiar to martial artists and non-martial artists alike. Through the silver screen, Chuck Norris gained millions of eager fans and has become a hero in the hearts and minds of our young people today. *Karate's Modern Masters* is a showcase in which these new masters present their specialties. Within these pages are the favorite techniques of established traditional masters, the new American breed of

masters, as well as the superstars of tomorrow.

The material is gathered from the pages of *Official Karate* magazine, the widest-circulating martial arts publication in America. With its staff of experts like editor Al Weiss and managing editor Alan Paul, *Official Karate* has served as a medium for the growth of karate in the United States. The magazine was founded in 1968 by Al Weiss, one of the few editors who also holds a legitimate black belt, under John Kuhl of New York City. Month after month, *Official Karate* brings us a good cross section of the multifaceted world of karate. With articles on traditional karate values, nutrition, physical fitness, and even full-contact reports, *Official Karate* is indeed the bible of American karate.

In order to cover the many facets of karate practice, we have segmented the book into four parts: history, kata, free-fighting, and weapons. They represent the most important branches of the art of karate.

The history section details the general history of the art, as well as exclusive coverage of karate in America. The sections on free-fighting, kata, and weapons, all contain the favorite fighting techniques of todays established superstars, and up-and-coming stars of tomorrow. Each chapter highlights the specialty of a martial artist, for example, Chuck Norris on hand techniques, Bill Wallace on kicks, Joe Lewis for redesigned techniques and so on. Ultimately, our selection of the martial artist was based on the credentials of each individual (traditional certification, belt degrees, karate titles, etc.).

The chapters will then complete a detailed section in the book, whether kata, free-fighting or weapons. Each section is as complete as possible making them an excellent self-study course for the beginner or advanced karateka (karate practitioner).

A NOTE ON USING THIS BOOK

To get the most out of this book, you should have some knowledge of karate basics. This doesn't mean you must be an expert—in fact, novices can benefit from this information as well—but *Karate's Modern Masters* has been written for those with prior experience in the art. For this reason, this manual does not present the basic techniques of karate, but instead looks at karate's four main branches: kata (formal exercises), free-fighting, self-defense, and weapons.

Novices will find the following books useful references to the basics.

Funakoshi, Gichin. *Karate-do Kyohan*. Tokyo: Kodansha Co., Inc., 1974.

Ivan, Dan, and Demura, Fumio. *Street Survival*. Tokyo: Japan Publications, Inc., 1979.

Nakayama, Masatoshi. *Best Karate: Vol. 1–8*. Tokyo: Kodansha Co., Inc., 1979.

Nakayama Masatoshi. *Dynamic Karate*. Tokyo: Kodansha Co., Inc., 1966.

Oyama, Mas. *Mastering Karate*. New York: Grosset and Dunlap, 1982.

Parulski, George R., Jr. *Art of Karate Weapons*. Chicago: Contemporary Books, Inc., 1984.

Exotic Weapons of the Samurai. Boulder, Colorado: Paladin Press, 1985.

Karate Power. Chicago: Contemporary Books, Inc., 1985.

Sword of the Samurai: A Manual of Japanese Swordsmanship. Boulder, Colorado: Paladin Press, 1985.

PART

I

HISTORY

CHAPTER 1
THE HISTORY OF TRADITIONAL KARATE

There is undoubtedly some truth to the notion that, since the very first conflict between men, we have had a desire to become formidable in skills of offense and defense. This need to dominate, or to prevent domination, weaves itself through the history of humankind so that our record is measured by our struggles against one another and is punctuated by the ever spiraling developments in weapons and strategy. Proficiency in unarmed combat has had its place within this hierarchy.

The oldest records we have concerning unarmed combat are hieroglyphics from the Egyptian pyramids. Egypt's military men, in about 4000 B.C., used fighting techniques that resemble modern boxing. Additional pictures representing something like boxing and wrestling turn up in the ruins of Sumer in Mesopotamia (about 3000 B.C.) and in the remains of Bein Hasan in Egypt (about 2300 B.C.).

These fighting techniques crossed over to Greece by way of Crete, and we find them described by Homer in the 23d book of the *Iliad*. Competitions in those days, it seems, were very rough affairs. Most of them ended in the death of one of the contestants because of the brutality of the techniques. According to one account, Theogenes, a fighting champion of the fifth century B.C., knocked out some 2,102 opponents, of whom 1,800 died. Another example was Milton, the greatest of Greek fighters, who carried a bull once around the Olympia Stadium, killed it with a single blow, and then ate it all himself.

In these early times there was a distinct difference between boxing arts and wrestling arts. Some individuals, however, combined the two types of fighting and developed the pancratium, in which everything was legal against an opponent, so long as it worked to take him down; thus the entire body served as a weapon.

Though the Greeks eventually found the pancratium too cruel, it was revived during the Roman Empire and perfected to a great degree. The art still exists today and has a small following in the United States.

Many believe that the first true form of karatelike techniques came from India. Although few documents exist, numerous statues dating back as far as the first century

B.C. depict temple guardians in poses similar to those used in modern-day karate. Further, legend has it that long before the first century the Kshatriya warriors of India practiced a native fighting art called *vajramushsti* which was mastered by warrior and priest alike. Several Indian Buddhist documents record three types of combat: reverse techniques, exchange of blows, and combined strikes.

The founder of Zen Buddhism, Bodhidharma, carried Indian fighting methods to China, where later students combined the art with native *chuan-fa* and developed numerous styles of combat, commonly called kung-fu today.

THE CHINESE FIGHTING TECHNIQUES

The first reliable records of kung-fu were found on bones and turtle shells of the Shang Dynasty (1766–1122 B.C.), although it is believed that kung-fu existed long before that. Chuan-fa, or fist way, as kung-fu was referred to in its early days, became very popular when the warlike men of Chou from western China defeated the Shang Dynasty ruler in 1122 B.C. During the Chou period, a kind of wrestling called *jiaoli* was listed as a military sport alongside archery and chariot racing. Chuan-fa continued to grow through the centuries and was called different names at different times. The next great development came during the Northern and Southern Dynasties (581–420 B.C.). During this era, the main regime began attacking the central area of China, and social order was greatly disrupted. This created an increasing interest in religious studies, as is historically the case during periods of war. Consequently, many religious figures entered the country. One was Bodhidharma.

Bodhidharma is an obscure figure in the history of Buddhism. The most reliable sources of our knowledge of the man are *Biographies of the High Priest*, by Priest Tao-hsuan (A.D. 654), and *The Records of the Transmission of the Lamp*, by Priest Tao-yuan (A.D. 1004).

These seemingly authentic sources notwithstanding, either modern scholars have been reluctant to accept any single version of Bodhidharma's existence or they assert that Bodhidharma is a legend. Many Buddhists as well as martial arts historians, however, have labeled Bodhidharma the 28th patriarch of Buddhism, assuming proof of his existence.

According to legend, Bodhidharma (also called Tamo, Dharuma, Dharuma Taishi, among other names) was the third child of King Sugandha of southern India, was a member of the Kshatriya, or warrior caste, and spent his childhood in Conjeeveram (also Kanchipuram or Kancheepuram), the small Buddhist province south of Madras. He received his training in Buddhist meditation from his master Prajnatara, who was responsible for changing the young disciple's name for Bodhitara to Bodhidharma.

Bodhidharma was an excellent pupil and soon surpassed his fellow students. By middle age he was already considered a Buddhist master. When Prajnatara died, Bodhidharma set sail for China. Three possible reasons are given for this: it was a deathbed wish from his master, Prajnatara; Bodhidharma was saddened by the decline of true Buddhism outside of India; or Bodhidharma was aware of the need for religious guidance in China and decided to make a name for himself by teaching in that country.

Regardless of the reason, it is believed that Bodhidharma arrived in China somewhere between A.D. 483–527. It is believed he first arrived in Canton and then traveled north, meeting Emperor Wu of the Liang Dynasty (A.D. 502–557) at Ching-ling (now Nanking).

When Wu (also called Wu-ti) saw Bodhidharma, he said "I have brought the Buddhist scriptures from your country to mine. I have built temples of great beauty and have seen to it that all under me learn the great Buddhist doctrines. What rewards will I receive in the next life for this?"

Bodhidharma replied, "None!" (Buddhists believe that when you do something expecting a reward, you can expect nothing.)

The emperor was so angered by this conversation that he banished Bodhidharma from the palace. Bodhidharma continued to travel to the north, to the Honan province, crossing the great Yuang-tse River on a reed, according to legend. He settled at the Shaolin (also Sil-lum) monastery on Mt. Shao-shih in the Sung Mountains.

After arriving at the Shaolin temple he meditated in front of a wall for nine years. Legend has it that during his meditation he fell asleep. He was so angered with himself that he cut off his eyelids and threw them to the earth. Where they fell, the tea plant was born. The leaves of the plant, of course, are used in a brew to combat sleepiness.

In his meditation, Bodhidharma founded *Ch'an* (Zen) Buddhism. Legend says that, in addition to Ch'an, Bodhidharma also founded kung-fu. However, as we have seen, kung-fu existed in China long before Bodhidharma.

It is more likely that, being a monastery, Shaolin housed many fugitives from justice, fugitives who were also skilled warriors turned monks. However, it is believed that Bodhidharma founded a series of exercises that helped unite the mind, spirit, and body— exercises that the warring monks found beneficial to their training. Two famous classics, the *Sinew Change Classic* and the *Washing Marrow*, were believed to have been written by Bodhidharma or by his followers, based on his teachings. From these classics came fighting applications in the form of the rock fist and the 18 hands of *lo-han*. During this time, the martial arts of China separated into two distinct forms: internal/soft boxing (*nei chia*) and external/hard boxing (*wai chia*).

KARATE IN OKINAWA

Most agree that karate, as we know it today, is a product of Okinawa, and Okinawa owes its martial heritage to China.

The history of Okinawa has been one of chaos. Located between the two great Asian powers, Japan and China, Okinawa has sometimes been devastated and greatly influenced by the tide of history and military conflict.

Okinawa first established cultural relationships with China in 1372. During this time 36 families came from China to live in Okinawa and establish diplomatic relationships. Many things were introduced, including chuan-fa (kung-fu). This cultural relationship was a product of King Satto (also know as King Shuten). King Satto was a wise king in military matters, and during his reign many castles and fortifications were built. Under his rule cultural relationships were extended to Korea, Arabia, Java, Sumatra, and Malacca. Many believe that *su-bak* (a Korean martial art) and Siamese empty-handed arts entered the country at this time.

In 1470 King Hashi took the throne. One of the first things he did was to restrict private ownership of weapons. Weapons were to be stored in a government warehouse under the direct supervision of the king. As a result of this law, empty-handed martial arts, both native and foreign, flourished.

In 1600, Ieyasu Tokugawa began the Tokugawa (Edo) period (1600–1853). Tokugawa became Japan's *shogun* (military dictator) and ruled the entire country with Buddhist and Confucian ethics. This era brought unification and peace to Japan.

Tokugawa lived by this rule: Where there is unity, there is strength; where there is division, there is weakness. Tokugawa maintained a strong hold on the country by keeping the *daimyo* (powerful feudal land owners) weak. He did this by forcing them to spend a portion of each year at Edo (now Tokyo). To assure their cooperation, Tokugawa kept the families of these daimyo as "guests."

The Satsuma clan from Shimatsu province were powerful rivals of the Tokugawa regime. The Satsumas tried to unseat the shogun but were unsuccessful. In 1609, to relieve the frustrations of the Satsuma warriors (and to prevent further war), Tokugawa handed over to them the island of Okinawa.

Under Japanese control, the Okinawans could develop no martial arts, and the ban on weapons was enforced with the penalty of death.

Native fighting arts such as *tode* resurfaced to aid the Okinawans. In addition, their interest in the Chinese martial arts traditions grew. In 1761 a Chinese military official entered Okinawa. Kusanku, an expert in chuan-fa, was sent by his government to teach the Okinawans his art, which consisted mainly of jumps, punches, kicks, and blocks but no kata, or formal patterned exercises.

Years later, Tode Sakugawa, who studied under Kusanku; Kung Syang from China;

and Peichin Takahara, a famous warrior of the native Okinawan fighting art of tode, blended chuan-fa with tode. Together they bore the name Okinawa-te (Okinawa hand).

Sakugawa was asked by Sofuku Matsumura to teach te to his son Sokon, who is credited with having made one of the single most important contributions to Okinawa's martial arts: the formation of the kata, prearranged karate dances that contain in them all the moves and secrets of the art.

Te developed differently in Okinawa, depending on its location and its emphasis. Styles emerged in the three major cities.

The te that developed in the city of Shuri became *Shuri-te* and emphasized external principles of speed, flexibility, and power. This style later developed into today's Shorin-ryu, *shorin* being the Japanese term for Shaolin ("young forest").

In Naha, *Naha-te* was practiced, with emphasis on the internal principles such as *ki* (spirit), breathing, coordination, and internal power. This style later developed into *Goju-ryu* (hard/soft school).

In Tomari, *Tomari-te*, emphasized both internal and external. Tomari-te, however, has passed into antiquity.

In honor of the fact that Okinawa's martial heritage was a product of Chinese influence, the Okinawan masters adopted the name *karate-jutsu*, translating as the "art of T'ang hand;" referring to the T'ang Dynasty of China.

It was in the twentieth century that karate entered Japan due to the influence of Gichin Funakoshi, considered the "father of Japanese karate." In the years following Funakoshi's arrival in Japan, other styles of karate-jutsu were developed. Many Okinawan masters brought their styles to Japan, among them Kenwa Mabuni, who introduced *Shito-ryu* in 1930, and Chojun Miyagi, who combined hard Okinawan karate with soft Chinese chuan-fa and invented the art of Goju-ryu. Other styles include Master Otsuka's *Wado-ryu* ("way of harmony"), considered one of the purest forms of Japanese karate, mixing karate with jujutsu techniques, and Mas Oyama's *Kyokushinkai-kan* a rough-and-tumble style mixing Shotokan with Goju-ryu (along with Chinese influence).

Karate-jutsu had become very much "Japanese," with all the customs and *reishiki* (etiquette) associated with jujutsu and *ken-jutsu* (swordfighting). Because of this, Master Funakoshi changed the concept of *kara*, which was originally written to mean "T'ang," and substituted another ideogram, also pronounced *kara* but meaning "empty"—thus, empty-hand art. Two years later, in 1935, Funakoshi discarded the suffix *jutsu* in favor of *do*, meaning "way," and karate-do was born in Japan.

Funakoshi's style of karate-do was called *Shotokan*, *shoto* being Funakoshi's pen name and *kan* meaning school. Shotokan is the largest system of karate in the world. The other major styles are Goju-ryu, Shito-ryu, and Wado-ryu.

In 1935 karate men from all over Japan formed a committee that solicited funds to build the first freestanding karate *dojo* (school). Construction on the building began in 1935 and was completed in 1936. Gichin Funakoshi, at the age of 68, bowed and entered the first karate dojo ever built. In honor to him, the karate men hung a plaque on the door of the dojo reading: *shoto-kan*, or the "hall of Shoto [Funakoshi's pen name]."

By 1940, with Japan engaged in war, the dojo was filled with eager young men wanting to learn the art. Following Japan's attack on Pearl Harbor, Funakoshi's dojo was literally overcrowded. After the defeat of Japan, many Americans began to study the art at the "hall of *Shoto*."

In 1949, Funakoshi's students organized themselves and officially adopted the name *Nihon Karate Kyokai*, or the famous Japan Karate Association (JKA), and named Funakoshi their chief instructor. Kichinosuku Takagi, a JKA instructor and judo black belt, founded the *Dai-Nippon Seibukan Budo/Bugei-kai* (All-Japan Seibukan Martial Arts and Ways Association), an organization that accepts martial arts for the sake of brotherhood.

By the late 1940s karate had found its way to America, as servicemen trained in Japan returned home from the war. In the late 1950s and early 1960s karate had become a recognized American activity with its own group of styles and heroes.

CHAPTER 2
KARATE IN AMERICA

To trace the roots of karate in the United States is not an easy task since the history is tied in with individual styles. A complete account including all systems, would take many volumes. Therefore, this chapter is a basic history detailing the introduction of karate to the United States and how it reached its present condition.

Empty-handed fighting arts, those that involve striking/kicking as their specialty, first reached the shores of the United States in the mid-1800s with the first Chinese immigrants. Kung-fu, the grandfather of karate, was an important part of the life-styles of the coolies—a term used to describe Chinese railroad workers during the frontier days of the Old West. The Central Pacific Railroad was responsible for the importation of the coolies, and by 1863 the swelling Chinese community actually isolated itself from the rest of American life and started its own subculture. As for most immigrants in the United States, this had its good and bad aspects, the good being a sense of community awareness and the bad being the influx of organized crime. The Chinese had their own crime syndicates, called the "Tongs," and up until 1930 the Tongs controlled prostitution, gambling, and other illegal acitivities within the community. The main fighting man during the Tong war years was called a hatchetman, because he used axe-weapons as his tool of death. In addition to the axe, the hatchetman was a skilled kung-fu fighter.

Karate was introduced to the United States not on the mainland but on Hawaii. Hawaii was and still is a center for karate activity, which began in 1927 when Master Kentsu Yabi introduced Shuri-te in a public demonstration at the Nuuana YMCA in Honolulu. In addition to Yabi, other Okinawan masters visited and taught in Hawaii. One of the most famous was Master Chojun Miyagi, the founder of Goju-ryu karate, who, on the invitation of a Hawaiian newspaper editor, taught karate for a year and returned to Okinawa in 1935.

Interest in karate was firmly established, and in 1942 James Mitose, a Japanese-American born in 1916 and trained in *kempo* (a Japanese term for kung-fu) in Japan, opened one of the first karate clubs, called the Offi-

Mas Oyama is the founder of the Kyokushinkai-kan system of karate. He is most noted for his exceptional power. To test his power, Oyama has confronted and killed, bare-handed, bulls marked for slaughter.

cial Self-Defense Club, located at Betetania Mission in Honolulu. Mitose's most famous students were Master Young, William Chow, Paul Yamaguchi, and Ed Lowe.

Of his students, Master Chow made perhaps the greatest impact on karate in Hawaii. Although Chow was a black belt in kempo, he decided to teach and call his art *kenpo*, meaning "first law."

Chow had many famous students, but the most important were Ardiano Emperado and Ed Parker, an American karate pioneer.

Emperado went on to cofound the *Kajukenbo* style of martial arts with four other experts: Walter Chou (karate), Joe Holke (judo), Frank Ordonez (jujutsu), and Clarence Chang (Chinese boxing). The name of their style is an acronym derived from the five disciplines of its founders: *ka* from karate, *ju* from judo/jujutsu, *ken* from kenpo, and *bo* from Chinese boxing.

Although Ed Parker was one of the first people to teach karate in the mainland United States, he was predated by Master Robert Trias, called by many the "father of American karate." Trias opened the first karate school in America in 1946 in Phoenix, Arizona. Trias trained with Tong Gee Hsiang, of the *Hsing-i* kung-fu (internal system) and was a student of Choki Motobu of the *Shuri tode-ryu* a style of *Shorei-ryu* karate. In 1948 Master Trias founded the United States Karate Association, the first organization of its type in America.

Ed Parker began teaching publicly on the mainland in 1954 at Brigham Young University. His evening classes, open to the general public, attracted a large following and a broad cross section of people. The class was attended by city police, students, housewives, game and fish wardens, and sheriff's deputies.

In 1955 Tsutomu Oshima, a graduate of Waseda University in Japan, traveled to the United States and opened a small Shotokan karate club in Los Angeles at the Konku Shinto Church. Oshima was a direct student of Master Funakoshi, and he is credited as being the first person to introduce a purely Japanese karate style to America.

In 1956 Ed Parker began to look for bigger and better things. He felt the best place to do this was the glittering West Coast, so in that

year Parker picked up and left for California. Parker quickly established a good reputation, and it wasn't long before he became the teacher of the silver screen stars. His list of students included Darren McGavin, Joe Hyams (an author), Tom Tannenbaum (television executive), Blake Edwards (a movie producer), and even Elvis Presley, one of the few Hollywood personalities to achieve the rank of a legitimate black belt.

It was right around this time that the general public began to notice karate, not through participation, but through its introduction on television and in the movies. The two earliest pioneers of karate in films were Ed Parker and Bruce Tegner. Parker managed to influence Blake Edwards to include karate-

Ed Parker is credited with forming the first commercial school of karate in America. A student of William Chow, he left Hawaii in 1951 and opened a school on the West Coast a short time thereafter.

type fight scenes in his movies, and this became a reality in 1960 in Edwards's films, *A Shot in the Dark* and *The Pink Panther*.

Tegner attracted attention to the martial arts with his series of some twenty-five books (many still in print) and by setting up fight scenes for the 1950s TV series "The Adventures of Ozzie and Harriet" and "The Detectives."

A British import, "The Avengers," which was introduced in America in 1964, starred Diana Rigg, a secret agent who was also an expert in martial arts. By the mid-1960s martial arts were a regular part of many TV programs. The most notable were "I Spy," starring Robert Culp and Bill Cosby; "The Wild Wild West," starring Robert Conrad, using karate/judo for fight scenes in each episode; and "Honey West," the first television show actually billed as a martial arts show, starring Anne Francis as a private investigator and judo expert.

However, the media saw the martial arts culmination in 1966 with the introduction of the "Green Hornet," starring Bruce Lee as Kato, who displayed weekly his brilliant style of kung-fu.

Although martial arts continued to appear on television and in the movies, the next big step came in 1972, when a television series called "Kung-fu" aired, with David Carradine as a Shaolin monk who, after murdering the Chinese emperor's nephew, immigrated to the United States. Caine, the main character's name, wanders the Old West, always knowing there is a price on his head. The greatest achievement of this long-running series was that it portrayed kung-fu as a philosophy and not just a fighting art.

In the same year the silver screen saw the introduction of *Billy Jack*, starring Tom Laughlin as a half-breed (American-Indian) war veteran who displays, in a spectacular fight scene, the Korean martial art of hapkido. Bong Soo Han, the fight scene coordinator, doubled for Laughlin in many of the fight scenes.

The success of *Billy Jack* and the TV series "Kung-fu" paved the way for the import of Chinese movies, especially those of Bruce Lee. The first import, however, was not a Bruce Lee film but a cheaply produced film titled the *Five Fingers of Death*. Bruce Lee's first

Benny Urquidez (right) is one of the most successful full-contact karate players in history. In addition to being a talented fighter, he has appeared in motion pictures (*Force Five*) and on television. Urquidez was featured in the TV documentary *The New Gladiators*, produced by the late Elvis Presley, himself a black belt.

Bill "Superfoot" Wallace (left) is most noted for his remarkable left leg kicks. Wallace has appeared in seminars in Europe, South America, England, and throughout the United States.

film release was *Fists of Fury* (originally titled *Big Boss* in China). Released in 1973, this film shows Lee winning freedom for himself and his fellow workers from illegal drug operations at a Chinese ice factory. His second film, *The Chinese Connection* (released in China as *Fists of Fury*), was also released in 1973 and depicts Lee attempting to fight anti-Chinese prejudice in Japanese-occupied Shanghai in 1938.

With *Enter the Dragon*, Lee's most professional effort, produced by Warner Brothers, martial arts became a worldwide phenomenon. Released in late 1973 (a few weeks after Bruce Lee's untimely death), the movie became an instant classic with sales grossing over $100 million.

THE EARLY KARATE PIONEERS

The core of karate in America was estab-

lished between the years 1956 and 1960 either by immigrating karate instructors from the Orient, or by U.S. servicemen returning from the war who had attained black belts during their stays in the East.

In 1957, Don Nagle, a U.S. serviceman stationed on Okinawa, returned to the United States and set up an Isshin-ryu karate school in New Jersey. Nagle was trained under the founder of Isshin-ryu, Tatsuo Shimabuku.

In 1957 Cecil Patterson a Wado-ryu black belt, returned to the U.S. and opened his school in Sevierville, Tennessee. Patterson was a remarkable businessman, and by 1975, he had opened 17 schools throughout the state. Patterson also authored one of the few books on his style in English, titled *Wado-ryu Karate* (Ohara Publications, 1975).

By 1958, George Mattson was discharged

from the U.S. Army. He returned home to Boston, bringing with him Uechi-ryu karate, an obscure but popular style of Okinawan karate stressing dynamic breathing. Mattson has also authored two major books on Uechi-ryu, *The Way of Karate* (Tuttle, 1969) and *Uechi-ryu Karate* (Peabody, 1985).

In 1959, Peter Urban opened his Goju-ryu karate school in Union City, New Jersey. Urban, a U.S. serviceman, studied in Japan under Richard Kim and Japanese Goju-ryu founder, Gogen "The Cat" Yamaguchi.

In 1960 Urban moved to New York City and opened his famous "China Town" dojo. At the same time, feeling that American karate should stand on its own, separate from the Orient, he established his American *Goju-kai* and announced his self-promotion to tenth-degree black belt.

Urban taught a number of influential ka-

Called the "father of Isshin-ryu karate in America," Don Nagle currently runs one of the most successful karate schools on the East Coast (Jersey City, New Jersey).

rateka, including Chuck Merriman, Frank Ruiz, John Kuhl, Aaron Banks, Ron Van Clief, and Owen Watson.

In 1959, Ron Duncan, a student of Don Nagel, began teaching karate and jujutsu in Brooklyn. In addition to combining karate and jujutsu, Duncan became one of the first to popularize martial arts weaponry on a larger scale. His seminars and demonstrations are as exciting today as they were 10 years ago.

Also in the late 1950s, Dan Ivan a CID agent in Japan for the U.S. government, opened up a successful school in Orange County, California. Ivan was one of the first Americans to receive judo training at the Kodokan and was also *the* first American to achieve the rank of black belt in aikido. In 1965 Ivan invited Fumio Demura, a Shito-ryu karate stylist who was also a national champion in Japan, to help him run his growing chain of dojos in California. Demura accepted the invitation, and today they run perhaps the most successful cahin of schools in the United States. Today, in addition to his movie efforts, Ivan is U.S.A. representative for the prestigious International Martial Arts Federation.

By now just about every major style of karate had found a home in America, and it was now time to expand the existing styles, especially Shotokan. Tsutomu Oshima arranged in 1961 to bring Hidetaka Nishiyama to California to run the West Coast operation. Nishiyama arrived in that year and in four months had parted ways with Oshima and formed his own Shotokan organization, called the All-American Karate Federation, a recognized branch of the powerful Japan Karate Association. The Shotokan pie was cut again in 1961 with the arrival of Teruyuki Okazaki, a Shotokan expert who began teaching in Philadelphia in 1962. He formed the East Coast Karate Association, originally intending it to be a branch of the All-American Karate Federation. However, he is now independent and represents the 50,000-member International Shotokan Karate Federation.

In 1961 John Kuhl started his own subsystem called *combat karate*. The effort began with the publication of a manual by the same title.

Considered by many to be one of the most controversial figures in American karate (because of his self-promotion to tenth-degree black belt), Peter Urban (right) is an American karate pioneer and a practitioner of exceptional skill and knowledge.

New York's Aaron Banks, a Goju-ryu karate black belt, is perhaps the most famous and successful promoter of martial arts events and tournaments.

Dan Ivan (right) learns a Nihon jujutsu technique from jujutsu, aikido, judo, and karate master Shihan Mochizuki. Ivan was one of the first Americans to teach martial arts to the public.

Kuhl, a student of Peter Urban and Gosei Yamaguchi (both Goju-ryu stylists, Yamaguchi being the son of the founder), went on to teach such notables as Aaron Banks and Al Weiss. In 1962, Kuhl and Weiss cowrote and produced a best-selling paperback manual titled *Karate*. This success prompted the first issue of *Official Karate* magazine, the most popular magazine on the East Coast today.

Upstate New York saw the opening of its first commercial martial arts schools in the early 1960s. This honor goes to two people: Frank L. Lane in the Rochester, New York, area (1961) and Peter Musacchio (1964) in the region of Syracuse, New York. Lane, a student from the Kodokan (judo); Masatoma Takagi (Shotokan/JKA); and Hironishi Saigo (Tenshin Shin'yo-ryu aiki-jujutsu) opened a true "martial arts center," teaching many different methods of martial arts. Musacchio, a sixth-degree Okinawan Goju-ryu renshi, operates the powerful CNY dojo in downtown Syracuse.

With motion picture and television successes like *Enter the Dragon* and the "Kung-fu" series, karate was well on its way to becoming big business. This came to a head when two brothers, Jim and Al Tracey, founded their first kenpo karate school in San Francisco. The Traceys, both students of Ed Parker, put up tremendous sums of money for development costs and launched the first franchised karate chain in America under the title Tracey's Karate. The chain became the largest group of schools in the world. The Traceys hired Joe Lewis, one of sport karate's brightest stars, as a figurehead for its recruitment program. As a result, their early instructors included such big names as Jay T. Will, Al Dacascos, and Steve La Bounty.

Others followed in the Tracey's footsteps, including karate and motion picture star Chuck Norris. Norris who first opened his school in 1963 in Torrance, California, expanded his operation to seven schools, which he gave up in 1975 to concentrate fully on his

KARATE IN AMERICA

An American karate pioneer, John Kuhl (center), packaged the first inclusive karate magazine, called *Combat Karate*. He also trained and promoted to black belt the coauthor of this book, Al Weiss.

Before retiring from active competition and becoming a world-class full-contact karate referee, Jay T. Will (right) was himself a karate champion. Will has starred in motion pictures and television. His most noted television role was on "Battlestar Galactica."

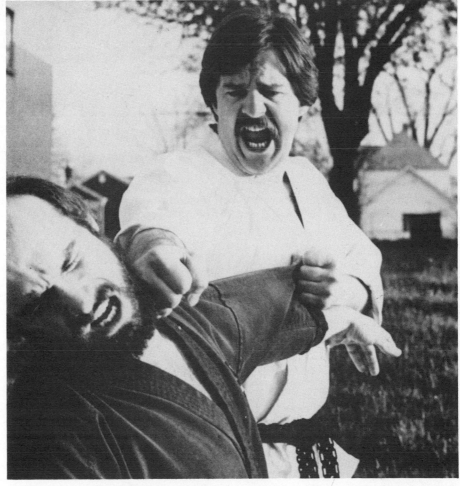

motion picture career. Among Norris's most successful black belts are Pat Johnson (who helped organize the 1984 box-office hit *The Karate Kid*), John Navidad, and Howard Jackson.

Indeed, karate has found a place in the hearts of Americans. Whether you point to the fact that ESPN (24-hour all-sports cable network) airs weekly professional full-contact karate bouts or that the second-highest ratings in television history go to the five-part miniseries "Shogun" (1980), focusing on the life of the Japanese samurai, karate has certainly become a part of American culture. It is for this reason that American karate instructors have begun to stand up and say, "Yes, American karate exists. We no longer need Japanese certification, for what we are doing is American." Needless to say, traditionalists say that this attitude is wrong, that only legitimate certification from Japan constitutes true karate. This can (and will) be argued for eternity. In the final analysis only one thing can be said: Americans have earned their right to stand up alongside their Japanese teachers as equals. And in the end, isn't this what karate is all about—brotherhood for the good of all?

A Japanese-born American karate expert, Hidy Ochiai is the founder of the Washin-ryu system of karate. He is most noted for his demonstrations of empty-handed kata and his performances with the sword.

PART II

KATA

To the uneducated observer, kata appears to be a dance in which the performer is striking and kicking at an imaginary opponent. In a sense, this definition is correct. However, it only touches on the basic concept of what a kata is.

What is the value of Kata? What exactly are kata?

Kata are organized sets of techniques performed alone in a special sequence against an imaginary opponent or series of opponents. These sequences cannot change; they must be practiced *exactly* as the masters have taught them or they lose their value.

Many students believe that kata training is nothing more than simulated fighting. As stated earlier, this is correct to a point. It is useful, when performing kata, to think of facing an opponent. However, it is useless to think that you might be confronted by a fighting situation in which you could perform a kata. Real opponents do not attack in prearranged patterns, so the response in a prearranged form (kata) would not be effective (except after decades of study). The ability to control body movement and the techniques learned through kata training are, however, very helpful in real fighting.

There are three important reasons for practicing kata. Firstly, they contain the basic body shifting, punching, and kicking techniques of the art, and by practicing the kata you practice the foundations of the art of karate. Secondly, practice of the kata for many years will eventually reveal to the karateka an inner core or secret technique embedded within the movements of the kata. Thirdly, the kata is a tool, like the postures of yoga, to transcend everyday activity. The kata promotes health (through physical fitness) and peace of mind (through the tranquillity achieved after years of kata training).

For one to learn kata he must observe and practice the movements. In Okinawa, where karate was used as a means of survival and teachers were scarce (see Chapter 1), the kata was a teaching tool. The sensei could put together a series of movements and teach them in an easy-to-remember, dancelike pattern. The student could then practice his art

17

alone, and when his sensei next saw him, he could test the student's progress by watching the kata. Although karate is no longer needed for survival, kata still is a very important means of testing a student.

The number of kata practiced in karate differs from system to system. Generally, it is acknowledged that there are 50 or so traditional kata in existence today. They range anywhere from as few as 25 moves to well over 200 movements. Kata are performed at predetermined tempos. The movements are a unique arrangement of fast-to-slow, slow-to-fast defenses combined with proper breathing, body placement, and focus (*kime*).

Kata have four points which are universal:

1. They begin and end on the same spot.
2. They have points of *kiai* (spirit harmony) at which the performer will shout to signify his determination and focus all of his mental, physical, and spiritual powers.
3. Kata repeat certain techniques, moving first in one direction and then in the opposite direction.
4. In most cases one major movement is repeated at least once in the kata. This is referred to as the *key movement*.

When learning a kata, you must first learn the actual techniques—the pattern of movements. This is best done by watching your teacher and taking notes.

Each kata has movement patterns. That is, you must perform each movement smoothly with no loss of balance and with complete control over yourself. This requires extra practice to master transitions between techniques and directional shifts in body weight.

The tempo and rhythm of the kata must also be learned. This is very difficult since the tempo often makes little sense to the beginner.

Each kata has points of kime (focus), where maximum strength and speed are exerted.

Kime, in the genuine sense of the word, is a trademark of a master.

Each kata contains *bunkai*, or the outward applications of movements. The outward applications are the obvious meanings or purposes of the movements; punches, blocks, and other techniques represent the same actions applied to a real opponent. Without application, the movements are nothing more than a dance. Bunkai make the training realistic.

Certain complex kata, in addition to bunkai, also contain *himitsu* or hidden-hand techniques. Himitsu were designed and built into the kata to preserve the deadly and secret techniques of a given ryu (school/style). The himitsu are not recognizable through casual observation; himitsu are movements whose meaning must be taught.

The inner, or spiritual, meaning of a kata must be experienced, not learned. This inner meaning comes as a realization after years of practicing a single kata—again, the trademark of a master.

How important are kata? In addition to everything that has been discussed so far, many masters believe that if you take the kata out of karate, you may still have a good fighting system, but it isn't karate. If you are just interested in fighting (only a fraction of karate's true meaning), there is nothing wrong with removing kata. Any good boxer or streetfighter can put a man down without the slightest knowledge of kata.

Streetfighting and karate training are distinct, however. As Mihagashi (a master of Goju-ryu karate) explained: "The man in the street lacks not only physical and mental discipline that comes from karate training, but also the finesse and definite refinement of form that can be achieved only through kata practice."

We have selected martial artists Frankie Mitchell, George Parulski, Jr., Peter Manfredi, and Frank Van Lenten to demonstrate the kata specialties.

FRANKIE "DR. SPEED" MITCHELL

GOJUSHI-HO KATA OF SHORIN-RYU

Frankie Mitchell, a student of Frank Van Lenten, holds black belt certification in Okinawan Goju-ryu karate, with extensive knowledge of Shorin-ryu karate. An avid tournament competitor, Mitchell was given the name "Dr. Speed" by his peers because of his speed and effectiveness with applying his techniques. Many years back, he and his uncle Richard Brookes formed the *Hatha Goju-ryu*—a traditional Goju-ryu system of karate with emphasis on yogic training and philosophy.

As a kata performer Mitchell has won local, regional, and national titles. His favorite and most successful kata for competition is the gojushi-ho form. It is also a representative kata of the Okinawan karate systems that exhibits fast/light movements (a trademark of the shorin-ryu system). Gojushi-ho has all the essential ingredients of the Shorin-ryu karate style and has been selected for this reason to appear in this section.

Mitchell teaches in Syracuse, New York, at the Dunbar Center, where he trains his special group of performers, The East Coast Demo Team (also known as the Spinning Cobras). He is coauthor of the book *Karate*

Power: Learning the Art of the Empty Hand, published by Contemporary Books, Inc.

GOJUSHI-HO KATA

1. **Ceremonial Opening.** Stand in open stance (hachiji-dachi) (photo 3-1). Step forward with right foot, extending both arms with palms downward (photo 3-2). Lift your right leg, extending your left hand and bringing your right fist to your chest (photo 3-3). Step forward into a front stance (zen-kutsu-dachi), delivering a right lunge punch (oi-zuki) (photo 3-4). Return right foot to form open stance (hachiji-dachi), clenching hands into fists and lowering the left while raising the right (photo 3-5). Open the right hand (photo 3-6), an action that symbolizes peace. Lower the right hand, which you reclench into a fist, and cover it with the open left hand at waist level (photo 3-7). This action represents strength governed by peace and wisdom. Raise your hands over your head (photo 3-8) and circle them around (photo 3-9) in a quick and forceful manner (photo 3-10) until they collide at chest level (photo 3-11).

2. Drop down, facing forward on left knee,

3-1

3-2

3-3

3-4

3-5

3-6

3-7

3-8

3-9

3-10

3-11

3-12

3-13

3-14

and execute X block (juji-uke) (photo 3-12).

3. Step forward to left front diagonal, forming a left front stance (zen-kutsu-dachi) and execute a knife-hand X block (shuto juji-uke) to the upper quarters (photo 3-13). With muscle tension and a slow movement, form the hands into fists (as if they were grasping an object) and draw them down to sides (photo 3-14).

4. Turn to upper right diagonal, forming a right front stance (photo 3-15). Repeat step 3 on right side (photos 3-16 and 3-17).

5. Step forward with left foot to left front diagonal, forming a horse stance (kiba-dachi) (photo 3-18). Opening the hands to knife-hand position (photo 3-19), execute a mid-level knife-hand inside-to-outside block (chudan shuto uchi-uke) (photo 3-20). In a series of *very* fast movements, shift weight to left leg, forming a left front stance (photo 3-21), and deliver a right reverse punch (gyaku-zuki) (photo 3-22), then a left straight punch (choku-zuki) (photo 3-23), a left front kick (mae-geri) (photo 3-24), and another right reverse punch (photo 3-25).

6. Repeat entire series of step 5 movements on right side (photos 3-26, 3-27, 3-28, 3-29, 3-30, 3-31).

7. Lift right hand (in knife-hand position) behind right ear (photo 3-32). Shift weight to left leg, forming a left front stance (zen-kutsu-dachi), at the same time executing an outside-to-inside knife-hand block (shuto-soto-uke) with right hand (photo 3-33).

8. Execute a backhand knife-hand strike (shuto-uchi) with right hand (photo 3-34).

9. Bring right leg behind left as you turn to face the rear, forming a cat stance (neko-ashi-dachi) and executing a low knife-hand block with left arm (photo 3-35).

At this point the camera turns to face the rear so you can see the detail of the action. Photo 3-36 shows the same movement as 3-35, except the camera is now at the rear.

10. Step forward (to rear) into a right cat stance (neko-ashi-dachi), executing a knife-hand block (shuto-uke) (photo 3-37).

11. Slide right foot forward into a right front stance (zen-kutsu-dachi) and execute a left reverse punch (gyaku-zuki) (photo 3-38). *Kiai* (shout)!

12. Turn 90 degrees to the front (clock-

3-15

3-16

3-17

3-18

3-19

3-20

3-21

3-22

3-23

3-24

3-25

3-26

3-27

3-28

3-29

3-30

3-31

3-32

3-33

3-34

3-35

3-36

3-37

3-38

wise) to face left side, forming a left cat stance (neko-ashi-dachi). At the same time, raise both arms in knife-hand formation in preparation for a block (photo 3-39). *Note: Camera, for this picture has once agained returned to face front.*

13. Without moving feet, snap the left hand into a low knife-hand block while the right hand holds the elbow of the left arm for extra support (photo 3-40).

14. Backstep the left leg behind the right, forming a hooked stance (kake-dachi), while delivering a ridge-hand strike (haito-uchi) with right hand and drawing the left hand to chest level (photo 3-41).

15. Step to the right with right leg, forming a straddle stance (shiko-dachi), at the same time delivering a double punch (morote-zuki) straight down (photo 3-42).

16. Lift your left leg to right, forming a crane stance (tsuri-ashi-dachi), while raising hands in guard position (photo 3-43).

17. Bring left foot down and form a right cat stance (neko-ashi-dachi), keeping hands as they were in step 16 (photo 3-44).

18. Snap the right hand down into a low knife-hand block (shuto-uke) while left hand holds the right elbow for support (photo 3-45).

19. Step over right foot with left, forming a crossed stance (juji-dachi) at the same time executing a rising knife-hand block (shuto age-uke) with right hand (photo 3-46).

20. Without changing foot position, lower right hand as if sweeping the blocked opponent's arm aside (photo 3-47) and deliver a powerful right-side thrust kick (yoko-geri-kekomi) (photo 3-48). *Kiai* (shout)!

21. Lower right leg, forming a right front stance (zen-kutsu-dachi), and deliver a left reverse punch (gyaku-zuki) (photo 3-49).

22. Swing your left foot to the rear, lowering yourself on the left knee, and execute an X block (juji-uke) (photo 3-50).

23. Stand up, bringing your right leg to the left, facing the right-side diagonal, and bring both fists to chest level (photo 3-51). Execute a double hammerfist strike (morote-tettsui-uchi) to each side (photo 3-52).

24. Bring your right foot behind the left,

3-39

3-40

3-41

3-42

3-43

3-44

3-45

3-46

3-47

3-48

3-49

3-50

3-51

3-52

3-53

3–54

3–55

forming an X stance (juji-dachi), while crossing both arms across the chest (photo 3-53). Deliver a double rear elbow strike (morote ushiro-hiji-ate) (photo 3-54).

25. Step forward with right leg, forming a right cat stance (neko-ashi-dachi), and exe-

cute a knife-hand reverse wedging block (shuto gyaku-kakiwake-uke). This action is done slowly with dynamic tension in all parts of the body (photo 3-55). *Kiai!*

26. *Closing the Form.* Repeat step 1 of the kata (opening the form) in reverse.

CHAPTER 4
GEORGE R. PARULSKI, JR.
KANKU-DAI OF SHOTOKAN KARATE WITH TIPS ON WINNING KATA COMPETITION

George R. Parulski, Jr., philosopher, martial artist, and author, began his martial arts career in 1963, studying judo under James D. Mounts and Shotokan karate under upstate New York karate pioneer Frank L. Lane, a seventh-degree black belt. Parulski holds a *yondan* (fourth-degree black belt) in Shotokan karate and a *godan* (fifth-degree black belt) in Juko-kai goju-ryu karate-do.

Parulski feels that the kata is the ultimate expression of karate as a martial art and as a mental/spiritual discipline. In the latter sense, the kata is a tool for achieving self-enlightenment, through which you learn your place in the universe and your limitations as a human being. Physically, Parulski feels that the kata is the essence of karate and that only through constant practice of kata can karateka even hope to master karate. Parulski competed regionally in kata between 1969 and 1974 and won numerous titles. His most recent win was a comeback effort in 1984, when he entered the American Karate Federation's Nationals and won first place in Master Kata and first place in Black Belt Weapons Kata (using a nunchaku).

Parulski feels however, his comeback effort was *not* a complete success: "The world of sport karate is very competitive. Many of the judges these days give stronger scores to those martial artists that deviate from traditional karate form, and change the purity of the kata in order to win a division. Only by adhering to the purity of karate can one hope to understand the vastness of the art."

The Sequences

Parulski demonstrates in this chapter the kanku-dai kata from the Shotokan system of karate founded by Master Gichin Funakoshi in the early part of the twentieth century.

Kanku (or "sky viewing") kata has two variations: *kanku-dai* (major kanku), and *kanku-sho* (lesser kanku). The kanku kata is a Japanese version of the Okinawa kusanku kata named after Master Kusanku (see Chapter 1). This kata is very old, and many other kata are derived from the movements within the kanku-dai form, including the Heian 1–5 forms, taught to all beginners up to black belt.

KANKU-DAI KATA

1. **Starting Position.** Assume an open stance (hachiji-dachi) with hands clenched in fists at your sides (photo 4-1).

2. Bring feet to closed stance (heisoku-dachi), bringing hands overhead and viewing the sky (meaning of kanku) through the opening formed by joining the thumbs and index fingers (photo 4-2).

3. Step out to side with right foot, forming an open stance (hachiji-dachi), at the same time snapping the hands apart (photo 4-3).

4. Step back with right foot, forming a right back stance (ko-kutsu-dachi), while blocking to the left side with an upper-level backhand block (jodan haisho-uke) (photo 4-4).

5. Turn to face right side, forming a left back stance (ko-kutsu-dachi), while executing an upper-level backhand block with the right hand (migi jodan haisho-uke) (photo 4-5).

6. Draw the right foot to left, forming an open stance (hachiji-dachi), drawing a left knife hand in front of the body (photo 4-6).

7. Execute a right straight punch (seiken choku-zuki) and then immediately, without hesitation, execute an inside-outside block (uchi-uke) with right arm while forming a left front stance (zen-kutsu-dachi) to left side (photos 4-7 and 4-8).

8. Return to open stance (hachiji-dachi) while executing a left straight punch (seiken choku-zuki). Without hesitation, execute an inside-outside block (uchi-uke) with left arm while forming a right front stance (zen-kutsu-dachi) to right side (photos 4-9 and 4-10).

4-1

4-2

4-3

4-4

4-5   4-6   4-7

4-8   4-9   4-10

9. Step forward with left foot, forming a right back stance (ko-kutsu-dachi), while executing a knife-hand block (shuto-uke) with left hand (photo 4-11). Look to rear and execute a right-side snap kick (yoko-geri-keage) while executing a right backfist strike (photo 4-12). Put kicking foot down and return to knife-hand block position (photo 4-13).

10. Step forward with right foot, executing a right knife-hand block (shuto-uke) (photo 4-14).

11. Step forward with left foot, executing a left knife-hand block (shuto-uke) (photo 4-15).

12. Step forward with right foot, forming a right front stance (zen-kutsu-dachi), while executing a finger thrust (nukite) with the right hand. *Kiai* (photo 4-16)!

13. Turn to face the rear (without any stepping movements). By turning you will form a left front stance (zen-kutsu-dachi). At the same time, execute a knife-hand strike with the right hand while placing the left hand, palm facing forward, at the level of your forehead. (photo 4-17).

14. Execute a right front kick (mae-geri) (photo 4-18).

15. Bring your kicking leg (right) to the left knee while turning to face forward. At the same time, deliver a right finger thrust (nukite) at groin level (photo 4-19).

4-11

4-12

4-13

4-14

4-15

4-16

4-17

4-18

4-19

16. Place the right leg back on the ground, forming a right back stance (ko-kutsu-dachi), while delivering a low block with the left arm and a high block to rear with the right arm (photo 4-20).

17. Shift weight to form a left front stance, facing forward. Repeat step 13 (photo 4-21).

18. Repeat step 14 (photo 4-22).

19. Repeat step 15, but turn to face rear (photo 4-23).

20. Repeat step 16 (photo 4-24).

21. Shift weight again to forward leg (you are facing rear), forming a left front stance (zen-kutsu-dachi) and delivering a groin-level finger thrust (nukite) with the right hand while bringing the left fist to the right shoulder (photo 4-25).

22. Repeat step 20 (photo 4-26).

23. Bring feet together and face rear. Look to left. Execute a side snap kick (yoko-geri-keage) while delivering a left backfist (photo 4-27). Place kicking leg down, forming a left front stance, and strike your left palm with your right elbow (photo 4-28).

24. Bring feet together, facing rear. Look to the right. Execute a right-side snap kick (yoko-geri-keage), simultaneously delivering a right backfist (photo 4-29). Place kicking leg down, forming a right front stance, at the same time striking the right palm with the left elbow (photo 4-30).

4-20

4-21

4-22

4-23

4-24

4-25

4-26

4-27

4-28

4-29

4-30

4-31

4-32

4-33

25. Turn to face left, forming a right back stance, while executing a knife-hand block (shuto-uke) (photo 4-31).

26. Step to the left rear diagonal, forming a left back stance, while executing a knife-hand block (shuto-uke) with the right hand (photo 4-32).

27. With right leg, step in a clockwise arc to face right, forming a left back stance (ko-kutsu-dachi), and execute a right knife-hand block (shuto-uke) (photo 4-33).

28. Step to rear right diagonal, forming a right back stance (ko-kutsu-dachi), and executing a left knife-hand block (photo 4-34).

29. Step to face rear, forming a left front stance (zen-kutsu-dachi), while delivering a right knife-hand strike and bringing the left hand, palm facing forward, above forehead (photo 4-35).

30. Deliver a right front kick (mae-geri) (photo 4-36).

31. Place kicking leg on ground and, a moment after it touches, snap the left leg behind it, forming a crossed stance (juji-da-chi). Simultaneously deliver a backfist with the right hand (photo 4-37). *Kiai!*

32. Step back with left leg, forming a right front stance, and deliver an inside-to-outside block (uchi-uke) with the right arm (photo 4-38).

33. Deliver a left reverse punch (gyaku-zuki) (photo 4-39).

4-34

4-35

4-36

4-37

4-38

4-39

34. Deliver a right forward punch (choku-zuki) (photo 4-40).

35. Spin counterclockwise 180 degrees to face front while executing an inside-to-outside scooping block (sukui-uchi-uke) with right arm and placing the fingers of the left hand at the elbow of the right arm (photo 4-41).

36. Bring right leg forward to the ground while lowering the body and looking straight ahead (photo 4-42).

37. Turn to face the rear, forming a right back stance (ko-kutsu-dachi), at the same time executing a knife-hand block (shuto-uke) with the left hand (photo 4-43).

38. Step forward (facing rear), forming a left back stance (ko-kutsu-dachi), while executing a right knife-hand block (photo 4-44).

39. With the left leg, step in a counterclockwise arc to face front, forming a left front stance (zen-kutsu-dachi) to left side, while executing an inside-to-outside block (uchi-uke) with the left arm (photo 4-45).

40. Deliver a right reverse punch (gyaku-zuki) to the left side (photo 4-46).

41. Turn to face the right, forming a right front stance (zen-kutsu-dachi), at the same time delivering a right inside-to-outside block (uchi-uke) (photo 4-47).

42. Execute a left reverse punch to the right side (photo 4-48).

43. Execute a right forward punch (choku-zuki) to right side (photo 4-49).

44. Step forward with left foot, forming a right back stance (ko-kutsu-dachi), executing a left knife-hand block (shuto-uke) (photo 4-50).

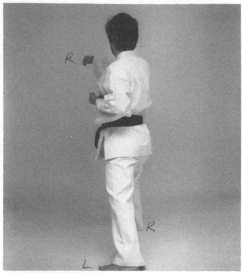

4-40

4-41

4-42

4-43

4-44

4-45

4-46

4-47

4-48

4-49

4-50

KARATE'S
MODERN MASTERS

4-51

4-52

4-53

4-54

4-55

45. Execute a right-side snap kick (yoko-geri-keage) to rear while simultaneously delivering a backfist with the right hand (photo 4-51).

46. Resume position in step 44 (photo 4-52).

47. Step forward with right foot, forming a right front stance (zen-kutsu-dachi), executing a right finger thrust (nukite) (photo 4-53). *Kiai!*

48. Step forward with your left leg, bringing it behind your right in a hooked stance (kake-dachi), at the same time bringing your right hand up near the back of your head (photo 4-54).

49. Pivot counterclockwise 180 degrees forming a horse stance (kiba-dachi) and deliv-

ering a hammerfist strike (tettsui-uchi) with the left hand (photo 4-55).

50. Execute a left backfist strike (uraken-uchi) (photo 4-56)

51. Strike your left palm with your right elbow (photo 4-57).

52. Bring your left fist to the left hip, placing your right fist above your left (photo 4-58).

53. Look to rear and execute a low block (gedan barai) with the right arm (photo 4-59).

54. Raise your right arm in the air, bringing your left leg to your right knee (photo 4-60). Pivot 180 degrees to face opposite direction, dropping down into a horse stance (kiba-dachi) and delivering a Y punch (yama-zuki) with both arms (photo 4-61).

4-56

4-57

4-58

4-59

4-60

4-61

55. With hands in tight fists, quickly (with a snapping motion) lower the right arm over left, executing an X block (juji-uke) at groin level (photo 4-62).

56. Open hands into knife-hand formation and raise them, executing a knife-hand X block (shuto juji-uke) at head level (photo 4-63).

57. Step around to rear diagonal 270 degrees, forming a right front stance (photo 4-64), while executing a knife-hand X block at head level (photo 4-65).

58. Execute a left front kick (photo 4-66).

59. Leap into air. As you come down, land on left foot and execute a right front kick (photo 4-67).

60. Place right leg down into a right front stance and deliver a powerful backfist strike (uraken-uchi) Kiai (photo 4-68)!

61. Closing the Form. Return to forward-facing position in a horse stance (kiba-dachi) (photo 4-69). Cross arms at groin level (photo 4-70) and circle them overhead (photo 4-71) and back to your sides (photo 4-72). Kata ends in open stance (hachiji-dachi) (photo 4-73).

4-62

4-63

4-64

4-65

4-66

4-67

4-68

4-69

4-70

4-71

4-72

4-73

Tips on Winning Kata Competition

1. Always present yourself to the judges in a confident manner. To do this, bow to the judges and state your name, style, teacher, and the name of the kata you are about to perform. Kata competition is judged like gymnastics, that is, a panel of 5–10 judges watch your performance and grade you on a scale of 1–10.

2. Be sure your *gi* (uniform) is clean and pressed. Make sure your school patches are sewn on straight. Your attire creates an image, and you want to appear professional in the judges' eyes.

3. Convince the judges that you are actually fighting an opponent when you execute the movements of the kata. This way you don't appear to be a robot acting out useless moves, but instead a karateka of high caliber.

4. Perform your kata *correctly*. To ensure that you perform it correctly, enter with a kata you are familiar with rather than one you have just learned.

5. *Eye contact:* Be sure to look in the direction you are about to turn instead of making blind movements. This way, you will appear to be actually fighting. Eye contact is essential to championship kata performance.

6. Be sincere in your movements. Put everything you have into the form.

7. If you make a mistake during the kata, do *not* let it break your concentration. Instead, continue with the kata as if nothing happened.

8. End your kata with the same determination and spirit with which you started it.

9. During *kiai* points in your kata, make sure your shout comes from the pit of your abdomen and that you shake the house with your piercing cries of combat.

10. Remember, you are always a winner if you give your kata 100 percent. Doing your best should be your goal, whatever the results may be.

PETER MANFREDI
KANKU-SHO OF SHOTOKAN KARATE

Peter Manfredi holds a *nidan* (second-degree black belt) in Shotokan karate under the Japan Karate Association and the All-Japan Seibukan Martial Arts and Ways Association (Dai-Nippon Seibukan Budo/Bugei-kai). In addition, he holds the prestigious titles of Certified International Instructor and *tashi* (expert) in karate.

Manfredi has competed successfully in kata competition on the East Coast and has elected to illustrate one of his winning forms. Kanku-sho, like kanku-dai, make up the most important katas in the Shotokan system, and is the second in the kanku series (kanku-dai being the first).

Manfredi was selected to illustrate this form because of his compatible body size for the form (short/heavy frame works best with the second kanku, while a light/thin frame works best for kanku-dai). He has also won numerous championships with his performance of this form.

The Sequences

Manfredi demonstrates the kanku-sho kata, the second in a series of two, the first being the kanku-dai (demonstrated by Parulski in the preceding chapter). Many believe that the kanku katas are the single most important katas in Shotokan karate.

KANKU-SHO KATA

1. Assume an open stance (hachiji-dachi) to start the kata (photo 5-1).

2. Step to left forming a right back stance (ko-kutsu-dachi), while executing an augmented forearm block (morote-ude-uke) (photo 5-2).

3. Turn to right, repeating step 2 on right side (photo 5-3)

4. Step to the rear with right foot, repeating step 2 straight ahead (photo 5-4).

5. Step forward into a right front stance (zen-kutsu-dachi) and execute a right lunge punch (oi-zuke) (photo 5-5). Immediately after punching, rotate fist so that palm faces upward (photo 5-6).

6. Step forward into left front stance (zen-kutsu-dachi) and repeat step 5 with left hand (photos 5-7 and 5-8).

5-1

5-2

5-3

5-4

5-5

5-6

7. Step forward with right foot, delivering a right lunge punch (oi-zuki) (photo 5-9). *Kiai!*

8. Turn to face rear, keeping feet in same position, and switch to a left front stance. With the left hand on the upper portion of the forearm near the elbow, rotate the right hand (which is in a knife-hand position) in one complete clockwise circle (photo 5-10).

9. Draw the right hand to right side, keeping left hand on forearm. This action is used to symbolize grasping an opponent's clothing and pulling him towards you. Deliver a right front thrust kick (mae-geri-kekomi) (photo 5-11).

10. Lower the right foot to ground and *very* quickly bring the left foot up behind the right, forming a crossed stance (juji-dachi), at the same time executing a backfist strike (uraken-uchi) with right fist (photo 5-12).

11. Step back with the left foot, forming a right front stance, while executing an inside-to-outside block (uchi-uke) with right arm (photo 5-13).

5-7

5-8

5-9

5-10

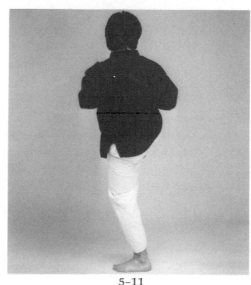
5-11

49

5–12

5–13

12. Deliver a left reverse punch (gyaku-zuki) (photo 5-14) and a right straight punch (choku-zuki) (photo 5-15).

13. Without stepping, turn to face the front, forming a right back stance (ko-kutsu-dachi), at the same time delivering a left low block and a right-rear-position inside-to-out-side block (photo 5-16).

14. In a very slow movement, bring your right forearm up and deliver a slow (with muscle tension) low block (gedan-barai). At the same time, slide your left foot to the right

into a T stance (teiji-dachi) (photo 5-17).

15. Slide your left foot forward into a left front stance (zen-kutsu-dachi) and repeat arm movement from step 8 (photo 5-18).

16. Repeat step 9 (photo 5-19).

17. Repeat step 10 (photo 5-20).

18. Repeat step 11 (photo 5-21).

19. Repeat step 12 (photos 5-22 and 5-23).

20. Repeat step 13, but turn to rear (photo 5-24).

21. Repeat step 14 (photo 5-25).

5–14

5–15

5-16

5-17

5-18

5-19

5-20

5-21

5-22

5-23

5-24

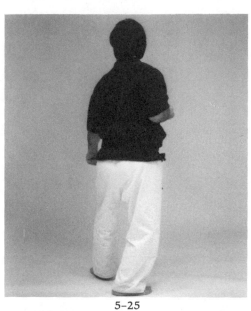

5-25

22. Step out with right leg, forming a left back stance (ko-kutsu-dachi), simultaneously delivering a low block with right hand and a high rear block with left hand (photo 5-26). Deliver a double punch to right (photo 5-27).

23. Turn to face left, forming a right back stance (ko-kutsu-dachi), and repeat step 22 on left side (photo 5-28 and 5-29).

24. Step forward (to rear) with right leg, forming a left back stance (ko-kutsu-dachi), at the same time placing your left hand above head, palm facing upward, and your right hand extended forward with palm facing upward (photo 5-30).

25. Leap into the air, spinning your body 360 degrees (counterclockwise) (photo 5-31). Full turn ends with feet in same position, except that you land facing the front in a knife-hand block position.

26. Execute a left-side thrust kick (yoko geri-kekomi) (photo 5-32). Place kicking leg down, forming a left front stance, and strike left palm with right elbow (photo 5-33).

27. Execute a right-side thrust kick (photo 5-34). Place kicking foot down, forming a right front stance, and strike right palm with left elbow (photo 5-35).

5-26

5-27

5-28

5-29

5-30

5-31

5-32

5-33

5-34

5-35

28. Step forward with left leg, forming a left front stance (zen-kutsu-dachi), and repeat arm movements in step 8 (photo 5-36).

29. Repeat step 9 (photo 5-37).

30. Repeat step 10 (photo 5-38).

31. Repeat step 11 (photo 5-39).

32. Repeat step 12 (photos 5-40 and 5-41).

33. Keeping feet in a right front stance, turn to face rear and execute a backhand block (haishu-uke) (photo 5-42).

34. Execute a right crescent kick (mikazuki-geri), striking left palm with right foot (photo 5-43). Leap into air turning 180 degrees counterclockwise, landing in a deep right front stance with both hands on the floor (photo 5-44).

35. Turn to face rear, forming a right back stance (ko-kutsu-dachi), and execute a left knife-hand block (shuto-uke) (photo 5-45).

5-36

5-37

5-38

5-39

5-40

5-41

5–42

5–43

5–44

5–45

36. Step forward to rear, forming a left back stance, and execute a knife-hand block with right hand (photo 5-46).

37. Pivot counterclockwise 270 degrees to face left side in a left front stance (zen-kutsu-dachi) and execute an inside-to-outside block (uchi-uke) (photo 5-47).

38. Step forward (to left) into a right front stance and execute a lunge punch (oi-zuki) (photo 5-48).

39. Pivot counterclockwise 180 degrees to face right in a right front stance (zen-kutsu-dachi) and execute an inside-to-outside block (uchi-uke) with right arm (photo 5-49).

40. Step forward (to right) with left foot, forming a left front stance, and deliver a left lunge punch (oi-zuk) (photo 5-50). *Kiai!*

41. Bring left foot to right, facing front in an open stance (hachiji-dachi), to end the kata (photo 5-51).

5-46

5-47

5-48

5-49

5-50

5-51

CHAPTER 6
FRANK VAN LENTEN
THE HIDDEN HANDS (HIMITSU) OF KATA

Van Lenten is truly an American karate pioneer. He was one of the select few to introduce karate to America after receiving a black belt rank while stationed overseas in the Marines.

Van Lenten holds ranks in Goju-ryu karate, Shorin-ryu karate, and kempo, which he learned in 1954 while stationed in Hawaii. He also studied Isshin-ryu karate under its founder, Tatsuo Shimabuku, in the 1960s.

Van Lenten is credited with being the founder of *Goshin-do* karate.

Currently he resides in Florida and is the U.S.A. representative of the Okinawan Shobukan Goju-ryu Association.

THE SEQUENCES

All kata contain both bunkai and himitsu and the distinction between the two is very subtle. Bunkai are those applications of the kata movement that are readily apparent. That is, a block and a punch in a kata are used to block an attack and counterpunch the opponent.

Himitsu, however are the hidden hands of the kata; they are applications that are not readily visible. These may include an arm movement that is really an arm lock and a body-shifting action that is in reality a throw when applied to an opponent. Since himitsu techniques must be taught by a certified teacher, those who are self-taught will not understand the application of certain steps in the kata. Consequently very few people are versed in the true meaning of the kata they practice.

Van Lenten demonstrates selected himitsu techniques from the Okinawa Goju-ryu karate kata called *saifa*.

In this chapter, each selected technique is shown first from the viewpoint of the actual kata movement. Next, the series is repeated, but with an opponent and, in some cases, with close-up photos to reveal the himitsu application.

6-1

6-2

6-3

6-4

SAIFA

Kata Movement 1

Assume a right hourglass stance (sanchin-dachi) and grasp your left hand with the right, locking palms (photo 6-1). Step back into a horse stance (kiba-dachi) while turning the clasped hands over and pulling them to your left shoulder (photo 6-2). Step forward with the left foot, assuming a right back stance and executing a knife-hand slash (shuto) to lower front with left hand (photo 6-3). Snap the left hand up into a ridge-hand strike (photo 6-4) and quickly shift weight forward into a left front stance (zen-kutsu-dachi), delivering a knife-hand strike (shuto) with right hand (photo 6-5).

6-5

6-6

6-7

6-8

6-9

6-10

6-11

Hidden Hands

Your opponent has seized your wrist and is attempting a wrist-twisting technique called a kote-gaeshi (photo 6-6). To escape it, you will use the hidden hand (himitsu) techniques found in the kata movements illustrated in photos 6-1 through 6-5. The kote-gaeshi (close-up photo 6-7) is a popular technique in aiki-jujutsu.

Clasp your hands (photo 6-8 and close-up photo 6-9) to prevent opponent from effecting wrist pressure and turn hands (photo 6-10), at the same time stepping back to release the hold (photo 6-11).

Step forward, delivering a knife hand to groin (photo 6-12), a ridge-hand to neck (photo 6-13), and a knife-hand strike to opponent's neck (photo 6-14).

6-12

6-13

6-14

Kata Movement 2

From kata saifa, assume a right cat stance (neko-ashi-dachi) and deliver a low forearm block with right arm while placing left fist under right elbow (photo 6-15). Open hands into a knife-hand position (shuto) and execute an inside-to-outside block (shuto-uchi-uke) (photo 6-16). Turn right hand into a fist (as if grasping clothing) and draw the hand to the middle of chest. Left hand becomes a fist and makes a small counterclockwise circle in front of chest; left fist ends up over the right fist (photo 6-17).

6-15

6-16

6-17

6-18

6-19

6-20

Hidden Hands

The following photos depict the hidden hand (himitsu) techniques found in the saifa kata movements illustrated in photos 6-15 through 6-17.

Opponent attempts a punch to the groin, which you block (photo 6-18). He immediately attempts a second punch which you block using a knife-hand inside-to-outside block (photo 6-19). Grasp the opponent's sleeve and draw the opponent toward you as you step forward (photo 6-20). Circling his left arm, deliver an elbow strike to your opponent's head and secure an arm lock to break your opponent's arm at the elbow (photos 6-21 and 6-22).

6-21

6-22

6-23

6-24

6-25

Kata Movement 3

From the saifa kata , assume a right cat stance (neko-ashi-dachi) and open hands to knife-hand position (shuto) with left hand at hip, palm up, and right hand over left, palm down (photo 6-23).

Step forward into a left cat stance (neko-ashi-dachi), and at the same time bring right fist to hip and left fist over right (photo 6-24). Lower your stance and circle arms around, smashing the right fist into the left palm (photo 6-25).

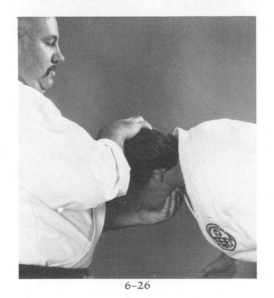

6-26

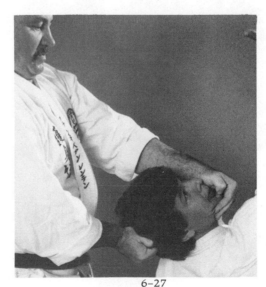

6-27

6-28

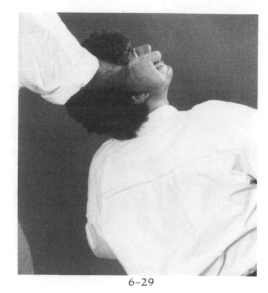

6-29

Hidden Hands

Here are the hidden hands (himitsu) movements found in photos 6-23 through 6-25.

Grasp opponent's chin with left hand and his hair with right (photo 6-26). Twist the head clockwise (photo 6-27), forcing the opponent to fall off his feet (photo 6-28). Before he can regain a stable position, crush his right temple with a right hammerfist (photo 6-29).

Kata Movement 4

From saifa kata, assume a left hourglass stance (sanchin-dachi), delivering a palm-pressing block (teishi osaekomi-uke) with left hand and a palm heel strike (teisho-uchi) with right hand (photo 6-30). Place right palm over left so that the palms face each other and assume a horse stance (kiba-dachi) (photo 6-31). Bring fists to their respective hips, bringing the right foot to left knee (photo 6-32). Step back down into a horse stance (kiba-dachi), delivering a double punch (morote-zuki) toward floor (photo 6-33).

6-30

6-31

6-32

Hidden Hands

The next photo sequence demonstrates the hidden hands (himitsu) movements from the techniques demonstrated in photos 6-30 through 6-33.

Opponent attempts a kick, which you block, delivering a palm heel strike to opponent's head with the right hand (photo 6-34).

With your left hand, reach under opponent's crotch grasping his belt (if no belt, then a handful of clothing). The right hand grasps opponent's shoulder (photo 6-35). Execute a scooping throw (sukui-nage), throwing opponent on his back (photos 6-36 and 6-37). Deliver a double punch to opponent's groin and neck, respectively (photo 6-38).

6-33 6-34 6-35

6-36 6-37 6-38

P A R T
III

FREE-FIGHTING

Free-fighting (*kumite*) is a training tool by which the basic techniques taught in the early stages of training and the complex techniques taught through the kata are put to the test.

Basically, free-fighting is an exchange of blows between one practitioner and another, in which one does not know what the other will do. The object is to make light contact with a clean technique to a vital part of the human anatomy. This is considered a point, and the one who accumulates the most points wins a match.

Free-fighting Divisions

There are several divisions in free-fighting (kumite).

Ippon Kumite (One-step Sparring). This is a training tool toward the more advanced free-sparring. In one-step sparring the partner attacks with one technique and you defend yourself with a series of techniques. The partner makes no attempt to block your techniques. The idea behind one-step sparring is to learn control coupled with effective combinations.

Nibon/Sanbon/Gobon Kumite (Two-, Three-, and *Five-Step Sparring).* These are progressive series of sparring drills in which the opponent attacks you with two, three, or five techniques. You step back and block each of his techniques and then counter with your own series of techniques. When you initiate the counter, no resistance is offered by the opponent. The object is to teach body movement and distancing techniques.

Jiyu-Kumite (Free-sparring). This is an all-out match in which anything goes *except* contact. The object is to score points and *not* to hurt your opponent.

Free-sparring should not be confused with the full-contact karate matches that recently became popular. This is a specialized field and does not come under the heading of free-sparring.

The following chapters in Part III represent the fighting techniques of today's favorite stars, such as Chuck Norris, Bill Wallace, Joe Lewis, Dan Ivan, and others. Each one demonstrates the specialty that took him to the top, either by displaying technique or by teaching a concept that will help you build good combinations for free-fighting on your own.

CHAPTER 7
CHUCK NORRIS
BUILDING EFFECTIVE COMBINATIONS

Chuck Norris is one of the greatest champions in the history of karate. In his competitive career (between 1965 and 1970) Norris won every major title and was undefeated when he retired from competition on January 17, 1970.

A graduate of the Lee Strasberg school of acting, Norris made his film debut in 1968 in *The Wrecking Crew*. In 1972 he costarred with the famous Chinese-American actor Bruce Lee in *Return of the Dragon* (released in 1974). In 1976 he starred in *Breaker, Breaker*. However, since Bruce Lee died, the public's interest in martial arts film has died with him.

Norris singlehandedly reinstated the interest in martial arts movies by convincing Hollywood filmmakers of their marketing potential. In 1977 he signed a three-picture contract and starred in *Good Guys Wear Black* (1978), *A Force of One* (1979), and *Octagon* (1980). In 1981 he starred in *An Eye for an Eye*, and in 1982 he coproduced one of his greatest hits, *Silent Rage*. During the same year he made box office success with *Forced Vengeance*. His most recent films are *Missing in Action 2* and *code of Silence* (both 1985).

Norris was named by *Black Belt* magazine to the Black Belt Hall of Fame in 1968 as "Player of the Year," as "Instructor of the Year" in 1975, and as "Man of the Year" in 1977. He also received a Golden Fist Award as "Outstanding Fighter of the Decade" (1960–70). He is the founder of the United Fighting Arts Federation.

THE SEQUENCES

In order to be an effective free-fighter, you must be able to develop effective fighting combinations. This is done through one-step-sparring (ippon-kumite). Norris, a *tang soo do* black belt (a Korean system), demonstrates how to build effective combinations by starting with a single defense and adding to it until it is a complex series of lightning-fast hand maneuvers.

BUILDING THE COMBINATION

Step 1: Knife Hand

Stand facing your opponent (man on left in photo) (photo 7-1). As your opponent steps forward with a lunge punch (oi-zuki), step to the side and block with a rising block (age-uke) (photo 7-2). Shift your weight forward and deliver a knife-hand strike (shuto-uchi) (photo 7-3).

Step 2: Knife Hand, Close Punch

Again, face your opponent (photo 7-4). As your opponent steps forward with a lunge punch (oi-zuki), step to the side and block with a rising block (age-uke) (photo 7-5). Shift your weight forward and deliver a knife-hand strike (shuto-uchi) (photo 7-6) and a close punch (ura-zuki) (photo 7-7).

7-1

7-2

7-3

7-4

7-5

7-6

7-7

7-8

7-9

7-10

Step 3: Knife Hand, Close Punch, Elbow

Stand, facing your opponent (photo 7-8). As your opponent steps forward with a lunge punch (oi-zuki), step to the side and block with a rising block (age-uke) (photo 7-9). Then shift your weight forward and deliver a knife-hand strike (shuto-uchi) (photo 7-10), a close punch (photo 7-11), and an elbow strike to the face (photo 7-12).

7-11

7-12

7-13

7-14

7-15

Step 4: Knife Hand, Close Punch, Elbow, Close Punch

Stand, facing your opponent (photo 7-13). As your opponent steps forward with a lunge punch (oi-zuki), step to the side and block with a rising block (age-uke) (photo 7-14).

Then shift your weight and deliver a knife-hand strike (shuto-uchi) (photo 7-15), a close punch (ura-zuki) (photo 7-16), a roundhouse elbow strike (mawashi-empi-uchi) to the face (photo 7-17), and a close punch to the ribs (photo 7-18).

7-16

7-17

7-18

7-19

7-20

Step 5: Knife Hand, Close Punch, Elbow, Close Punch, Uppercut

Now combine all the techniques for a final combination. This combination will deliver five counterattacks and must be done in less than two seconds.

Stand, facing your opponent (photo 7-19). As your opponent steps forward with a lunge punch (oi-zuki), step to the side and block with a rising block (age-uke) (photo 7-30). Now shift your weight and deliver a knife-hand (shuto-uchi) (photo 7-21), a close punch (ura-zuki) to the ribs (photo 7-22), a round-house elbow strike (mawashi-empi-uchi) to the face (photo 7-23), a close punch (ura-zuki) to the ribs (photo 7-24), and a final uppercut to the chin (photo 7-25).

7-21

7-22

7-23

7-24

7-25

CHAPTER 8
BILL "SUPERFOOT" WALLACE
USING THE LEGS EFFECTIVELY

Wallace held the title of World Professional Karate Middleweight Champion from 1974 (full-contact karate) until his retirement in the early eighties.

Wallace began his martial arts training in judo (1966) and then began karate when he served in the U.S. Air Force. His first instructor was Michael Gneck, a Shorin-ryu karate student, in San Bernardino, California. His next teacher was Glenn Keeney of Indiana. Wallace began studying under Keeney in 1968, and, although he did not adopt any of Keeney's Shorei-goju style, Wallace credits much of his sparring ability to Keeney's early training.

Wallace was named to the Black Belt Hall of Fame in 1978 as "Man of the Year" and also received awards twice as "Karate Player of the Year." A combination taekwon-do and Shorin-ryu stylist, Wallace is most noted for his left roundhouse and hook kicks. Many have commented that Wallace uses his left leg better than most use their right hand.

THE SEQUENCES

Wallace demonstrates in the following sequence how to use your legs effectively in a sparring situation. The key to good kicking ability says Wallace, is daily stretching. You should stretch slowly and without pain, holding the point of stretch for as long as possible.

SPARRING COMBINATIONS

Combination 1: Crossover Side Kick

Stand, facing your opponent (man on right in photo) in a ready stance (photo 8-1). Begin to shift your weight forward (photo 8-2) toward your opponent. Crossing your rear leg behind your lead leg (photo 8-3), throw a side kick to the face of your opponent (photo 8-4). *Note Wallace's style in this combination and those that follow—his side kick demonstrates perfect form.*

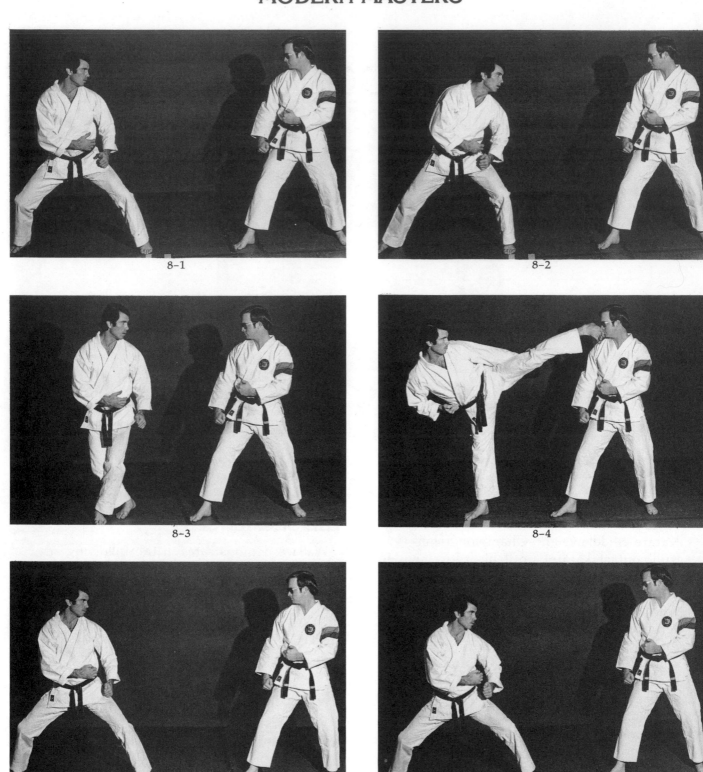

8-1

8-2

8-3

8-4

8-5

8-6

8-7

8-8

Combination 2: Skip Side Kick

An extremely fast kicking technique, this kick can be used equally well against an advancing or retreating opponent.

Stand, facing your opponent (photo 8-5). Now shift your weight forward (photo 8-6), bring your rear leg to your lead leg (photo 8-7) in a skipping action, and throw a side kick to the head of your opponent (photo 8-8).

Combination 3: Fake Side Kick into Backfist

Stand, facing your opponent in a ready stance (photo 8-9). Skip forward, bringing your rear leg to your lead leg (photo 8-10), and chamber your leg for a side kick (photo 8-11). Your opponent's attention is drawn to the chambered leg, creating an opening at his head. Bring your kicking leg down and execute a backfist to your opponent's face (photo 8-12).

The key to making this combination work is to convince your opponent you are really trying a side kick. Therefore, your heart and soul must be put behind the kicking action. Only at the last fraction of a second do you change intent and deliver the backfist.

8-9

8-10

8-11

8-12

Combination 4: Side Kick to Roundhouse Kick

Stand, facing your opponent in a ready stance (photo 8-13). Skip forward, bringing the rear leg to the lead leg (photo 8-14). Then bring your kicking leg into chamber position (photo 8-15) and deliver a side kick at opponent's head (photo 8-16).

Opponent leans out of range of the kick and intends to charge in to score on you as you bring your kicking leg down. Anticipating his charge, snap home a roundhouse kick (with the same leg that threw the side kick), hitting the opponent on the side of the head (photo 8-17).

8-13

8-14

8-15

8-16

8-17

CHAPTER 9
PETER MUSACCHIO
EFFECTIVE GOJU-RYU KARATE COMBINATIONS

Peter Musacchio is a pioneer of karate in America. He opened one the first karate dojos in the United States and *the* first on the East Coast in 1960. Returning home from the service with certification in Okinawan Goju-ryu karate, Musacchio now holds a sixth-degree black belt and the prestigious title of *renshi* or "polished expert," from Master Shinjo (Okinawan Shobukan Goju-ryu Karate Association).

Musacchio has always been noted as an effective combinations man, meaning he throws his techniques with the intention of creating an opening in his opponent's defense and scoring to that opening. Because of his exceptional skill at combinations and his legendary contributions to the art—as an American pioneer of karate—he was selected to appear in this section.

He lives in Syracuse, New York, where he runs the Central New York Karate Academy.

THE SEQUENCES

Musacchio's trademark is fast, effective, *traditional* combinations that are applicable on the street as well as in free-fighting. Here Musacchio demonstrates ippon kumite (one-step sparring) against a punch or a kick.

IPPON KUMITE

Combination 1

Stand, facing your opponent (man on right in photo) (photo 9-1). When opponent steps forward to punch, block the punch (photo 9-2) and deliver a counterpunch to opponent's rib cage (photo 9-3). Stepping around (photo 9-4) to the rear of the opponent (photo 9-5), secure a choke hold (photo 9-6) and take your opponent down to the ground (photos 9-7 and 9-8).

9-1

9-2

9-3

9-4

9-5

9-6

9–7

9–8

9–9

Combination 2

Stand, facing your opponent (man on left in photo) (photo 9-9). As opponent attempts a punch, you block the technique with your elbow as you turn sideways and sink into a horse stance (kiba-dachi) (photo 9-10). Grasping hold of the attacker's punching arm (photo 9-11), deliver four very rapid attacks: a backfist (photo 9-12), a vertical punch (photo 9-13), a palm heel (photo 9-14), and a knee to the groin (photo 9-15).

9–10

9–11

9–12

9–13

9–14

9–15

Combination 3

Stand, facing your opponent (man on right in photo) (photo 9-16). Opponent attempts a punch, which you sidestep. Grasping the punching hand (photo 9-17), deliver three very rapid kicks with the same leg: a cutting kick (fumi-kiri) to the knee (photo 9-18), a side-thrust kick (yoko-geri-kekomi) to the ribs (photo 9-19), and a roundhouse kick (mawashi-geri) to opponent's face (photo 9-20).

9–16

9–17

9–18

9–19

9–20

Combination 4

Stand, facing your opponent (man on right in photo) (photo 9-21). As opponent attempts a punch, block it with your forearm (photo 9-22). Grasping the attacker's punching arm, spin clockwise (photo 9-23) and, using your lead leg (photo 9-24), sweep the attacker's legs out from under him (photos 9-25 and 9-26).

9–21

9–22

9–23

9–24

9–25

9–26

Combination 5

Stand, facing your opponent (man on right in photo) (photo 9-27). Opponent attempts a front kick to the groin (photo 9-28). Block the kick, wrap your arm around the leg to trap it (photo 9-29), and grasp the opponent's lapel (photo 9-30). Then step in between opponent's legs and lift him off the ground (photo 9-31). End the defense by slapping the opponent's back into the ground and delivering a punch to the head (photo 9-32).

9-27

9-28

9-29

9-30

9-31

9-32

CHAPTER 10
JOE LEWIS
EFFECTIVE HAND TECHNIQUES FOR POINT COMPETITION

Born in 1944, Lewis joined the Marines in 1962 and first was exposed to karate while stationed in Okinawa. Lewis trained under the famed Shorin-ryu karate master Eizo Shimabuko and earned his black belt in an incredible seven months.

Back in the United States, Lewis soon became a point tournament champion and won every match he entered, garnering a total of some 30 major titles. He, along with Chuck Norris and Mike Stone, is considered one of the 1960's three great American champions.

In addition to Shorin-ryu karate, Lewis studied with Bruce Lee, learning his jeet kune do art, and from boxer Joe Orbillo (Lewis at one point considered entering the boxing ring).

He introduced full-contact karate in 1970, calling it *kickboxing*, and reigned as the U.S. Heavyweight Champion, defending his title 10 times. He was inducted into the Black Belt Hall of Fame in 1975 as "Karate Player of the Year."

Lewis conducts seminars nationwide and lives in California, where he is currently writing a book with John Corcoran called *Karate for the Masses*.

THE SEQUENCES

Lewis, in a classic series that appeared in the *Official Karate Yearbook*, demonstrates the hand combinations that won him fame.

HAND COMBINATIONS

Technique 1: The Jab (Kisami-zuki)

The jab is one of the most effective techniques in point combination. Delivered with power and proper focus, the technique will easily award you the point. It is also an effective fake in order to open up your opponent for a follow-up technique.

The Lewis method of throwing a jab is fast and effective. Starting from a solid ready stance (photo 10-1), lean forward with your hips (photo 10-2) and throw the jab to opponent's head (opponent is on left in photo) (photo 10-3). Note that Lewis has nearly fully extended his arm in the photo and does not turn the fist but instead keeps it vertical. Lewis believes this method is faster and, because the arm is extended, keeps the opponent a safe distance away.

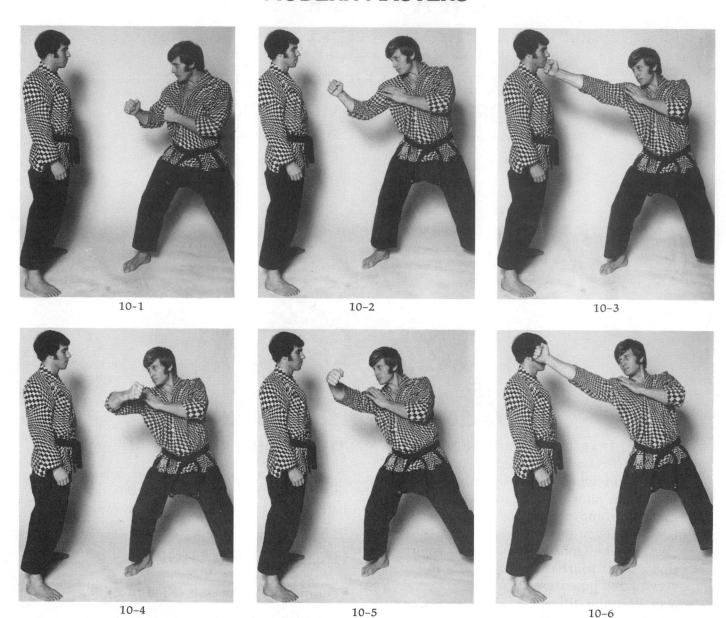

10-1   10-2   10-3

10-4   10-5   10-6

Technique 2: Back Fist (uraken-uchi)

The backfist may be the technique used most frequently to score a point in competition because it is fast and can be withdrawn quickly to protect yourself from your opponent.

Stand, facing your opponent (photo 10-4). As with the jab, thrust your hips and body weight forward (photo 10-5) and deliver the backfist to the side of opponent's head (photo 10-6). To regain a stable position, immediately snap your fist back into a guard position (photo 10-7).

The key points in the Lewis method are the lean forward into the striking action, the hip-thrusting action, and the snap-back immediately upon making contact with the target.

10-7

10-8

10-9

Technique 3: Close Fist or Uppercut (ura-zuki)

The close fist is traditionally a close range punch, but the Lewis method applies the technique at a distance.

Standing facing your opponent (photo 10-8), lean to the side (corresponding to the punching hand) as you deliver the closepunch (photo 10-9). As for the backfist, immediately snap back the punch (photo 10-10) to regain a ready position.

What is unique about the Lewis method is that he leans to the side before delivering the punch, and he punches at a considerable distance from his opponent.

Technique 4: Ridge Hand (haito-uchi)

The ridge hand is a powerful technique, but traditionally it is a slow maneuver, which has made it impractical for point competition. Lewis is credited with developing the ridge hand to a high degree, making it a useful tool for point play. Because of his pioneering efforts, the ridge hand today is one of the most frequently used techniques in competition.

10-10

Facing your opponent in a ready stance (photo 10-11), duck (as if evading an oncoming attack) (photo 10-12) and open your hand (photo 10-13). In a snapping action, deliver the ridge hand to the side of the opponent's head (photo 10-14) and immediately snap it back (photo 10-15).

Again, the trademarks of the technique are the snapping action and the ducking maneuver that precedes the technique's delivery.

10–11

10–12

10–13

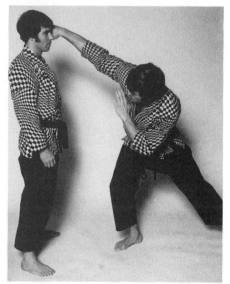
10–14

10–15

CHAPTER 11
MARK McCARTHY
THE DOUBLE KICK

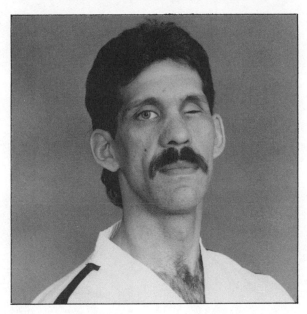

Holding the rank of fourth degree black belt in taekwon-do through the prestigious International Taekwon-do Federation, Mark McCarthy has acquired an impressive list of titles: (1) International Instructor (ITF), (2) Class A referee, (3) Secretary General of Taekwon-do Instructor's Association, and (4) Coach of the U.S.A. Taekwon-do team that competes internationally in ITF events.

Taekwon-do is noted for its impressive kicking techniques in which a practitioner can throw one, two, and even three kicks with the same leg. These double kicks are useful in free-fighting as well as self-defense situations. McCarthy, because of his exceptional ability in this system, was selected to demonstrate the "double kick."

McCarthy lives in Rochester, New York, where he runs his own school, the Taekwon-do Junshin—one of the most successful schools on the East Coast. He is coauthor of the book *Taekwon-do* with George R. Parulski.

THE SEQUENCES

The double kicks are used when the first kicking action does not make full contact with

the opponent's body because the opponent has made an evasive movement. The second kick, then, is a follow-up to the first kick.

Double kicking can also be used when you want to score a point with more than just one technique. Throwing many kicks at your opponent in rapid succession will achieve that goal.

DOUBLE KICK COMBINATIONS

Combination 1: Front Kick to Roundhouse Kick

1. Start by facing your opponent (man on right in photo) (photo 11-1).

2. Chamber your leg to begin your first kicking technique (photo 11-2).

3. Now execute a front kick, which the opponent avoids by leaning forward (photo 11-3).

4. Taking advantage of the opponent's facial opening, rechamber your leg (photo 11-4).

5. Finally, execute a high roundhouse kick (also called a *turning kick*) to the opponent's head (photo 11-5).

11-1

11-2

11-3

11-4

11-5

Combination 2: Double Roundhouse (Turning) Kick

1. Start by facing your opponent (man on right in photo) (photo 11-6).

2. Then shift your weight forward (photo 11-7).

3. Chamber your rear leg (photo 11-8).

4. From the chamber position, execute a roundhouse kick (photo 11-9).

5. Rechambering your leg (not illustrated: chamber is the same as photo 11-8), execute a high turning kick to your opponent's head (photo 11-10).

92

11-6

11-7

11-8

11-9

11-10

93

CHAPTER 12
RANDY PUMPUTIS
ISSHIN-RYU KARATE SPORT COMBINATIONS

Randy Pumputis is an East Coast karate champion in both kata and kumite. He has been rated by *Karate Illustrated* magazine as the number three fighter in region 11 (New York area) and has been successful in national events.

Pumputis holds a third-degree black belt in the Isshin-ryu karate system—a system noted for its simple, no-nonsense techniques. Pumputis's trademark in fighting is his ability to put together successful combinations, a skill that has made him one of the best fighters in the tournament circuit today. It is for this reason he appears in this chapter.

Pumputis lives in Greece, New York, where he operates the Pumputis Karate Academy.

THE SEQUENCES

Pumputis is noted for his effective leg tech-

niques and his combinations. His philosophy is to throw combination after combination, never giving the opponent a chance to move in on him.

Pumputis demonstrates in the following photos some of his more effective sport combinations.

SPORT COMBINATIONS

Combination 1: Side Kick to Ridge Hand

Stand, facing your opponent (man on right in photo) in a fighting stance (photo 12-1). To bridge the gap between you and your opponent, slide your rear foot up to your lead leg (photo 12-2) and deliver a side kick to your opponent's rib cage (photo 12-3). Placing the kicking leg down, follow through with a ridge hand to the opponent's face (photo 12-4).

12-1

12-2

12-3

12-4

12-5

Combination 2: Fake Backfist to Ridge Hand to Hook Kick

Face your opponent (man on right in photo) in a fighting stance (photo 12-5). Lean forward and execute a backfist at opponent's face (photo 12-6). The backfist draws the opponent's attention to his face level, leaving the midsection open. Take advantage of the opening and deliver a ridge hand (photo 12-7). Then follow up with a hooking kick (photos 12-8, 12-9, and 12-10) to opponent's head.

12-6

12-7

12-8

12-9

12-10

Combination 3: Backfist to Punch to Double Roundhouse Kick

Face your opponent (man on right in photos) in a fighting stance (photo 12-11). Start the combination with two lightning-fast hand techniques: first, a backfist to the head (photo 12-12) and, second a vertical punch to the midsection (photo 12-13). Finish the combination with a double roundhouse kick with the same leg, first to the midsection (photo 12-14) and then to the head (photo 12-15).

12-11

12-12

12-13

12-14

12-15

Combination 4: Sliding Front Kick to Reverse Punch to Roundhouse Kick

This is one of Pumputis's favorite combinations. Start the maneuver in a stable ready stance (photo 12-16). Charging in on your opponent (man on left in photos) skip your rear leg to the lead leg and chamber the front leg for a kick (photo 12-17). Zero in on the opponent's side and deliver a front kick (photo 12-18). The next two techniques are done *very* rapidly. As the opponent steps forward after your kicking action follow up with a reverse punch (photo 12-19) to the midsection and a high roundhouse kick (photo 12-20) to the head.

12–16

12–17

12–18

12–19

12–20

Combination 5: Hook Kick to Roundhouse Kick

This is a popular leg combination in tournaments. Pumputis feels that many players neglect the leg combinations in favor of the hands. This is a mistake because, according to Pumputis, the legs have as much to offer as, if not more than, hand combinations. Therefore, a true champion can mix combinations using his hands, feet, or both.

Start by facing your opponent (man on left in photo) in a fighting stance (photo 12-21). Bridging the gap between you and your opponent, slide your rear leg to your lead leg and chamber the lead leg for a kick (photo 12-22).

Execute a hooking kick to the back of your opponent's head (photo 12-23), bringing the hooking action through to a chamber position (photo 12-24). Execute a roundhouse kick at the opponent's head (photo 12-25).

12-21

12-22

12-23

12-24

12-25

CHAPTER 13
ED FOX
EFFECTIVE COMBINATIONS USING KUNG-FU AND KARATE

Ed Fox has trained with and received his black belt from Hidy Ochiai in the Washin-ryu karate system. He has also studied Ch'ang-ch'uan kung-fu under Tayari Casel and has received teaching credentials. Most recently he has attained certification in *kupiganangumi*, the rhythmic and acrobatic martial art developed by African slaves and their descendants. Kupiganangumi stresses ground fighting and Fox has successfully incorporated ground fighting tactics into his fighting style. Fox's fighting techniques have been featured in numerous magazine articles, and because of his unique ground fighting ability, Fox was chosen to show his skill in this section.

Fox teaches in Syracuse, New York, and is a member of the Syracuse Black Belt Council.

THE SEQUENCES

Fox demonstrates a number of sequences that are effective in sport play as well as in self-defense. He also demonstrates a unique style of ground fighting in which you must defend yourself after you have been knocked down.

GROUND DEFENSES

Defense 1

Opponent (man on left in photos) has knocked you down. He stands above you, ready to attack you again (photo 13-1). As he reaches for you, block his arms with your legs (photo 13-2) and, grasping his arm for support, deliver a kick to the base of his chin (photo 13-3).

13-1

13-2

13-3

Defense 2

Again, your opponent has knocked you down, and he stands above you (photo 13-4). This time, instead of reaching, as he tried in defense 1, he attempts to punch you. Block the punch with your leg (photo 13-5) and, using the same leg, deliver two rapid counterkicks—one to the face (photo 13-6) and the other to the ribs (photo 13-7).

13-4

13-5

13-6

13-7

Defense 3

Your opponent has knocked you down and has jumped at you to secure a choke hold around your neck (photo 13-8). Grasping his hands, apply a double wrist lock (photo 13-9) and counterkick the opponent on the base of the chin (photo 13-10). To finish him off, deliver a heel-stomping kick to the groin (photos 13-11 and 13-12)

13-8

13-9

13-10

13-11

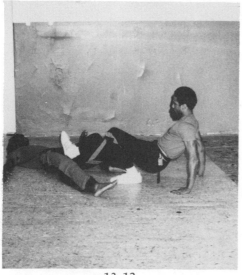

13-12

COMBINATIONS

Combination 1

Stand, facing your opponent in a ready stance (photo 13-13). As your opponent attempts a punch, duck to the side and under the punching action (photo 13-14) and deliver a ridge hand to the midsection (photo 13-15). As a finishing technique, sweep your opponent's leg out from under him (photos 13-16 and 13-17) and deliver a kick to his head (photo 13-18).

13–13

13–14

13–15

13–16

13–17

13–18

Combination 2

Stand, facing your opponent in a ready stance (photo 13-19). Your opponent attempts a punch, which you catch, then deliver a knife-hand strike to the punching arm (photo 13-20). Countering with a kick to the face (photo 13-21), finish the combination by twisting the opponent's wrist (photo 13-22) until it takes the opponent down (photos 13-23 and 13-24).

13-19

13-20

13-21

13-22

13-23

13-24

Combination 3

Stand, facing your opponent (photo 13-25). As your opponent chambers his leg for a kicking action (photo 13-26), fall to the ground (photo 13-27) out of the range of the kick and knock the opponent's support leg out from under him (photo 13-28). Counterattack with a kick to the groin (photo 13-29).

13-25

13-26

13-27

13-28

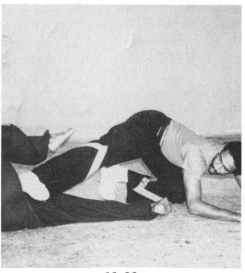

13-29

CHAPTER 14
SUK JUN KIM
ADVANCED TAEKWON-DO COMBINATIONS

Suk Jun Kim began his extensive training in Taekwon-do in 1963 in Seoul, South Korea. Currently, Kim holds a sixth-degree black belt in taekwon-do from the International Taekwon-do Federation (ITF) and is an international instructor and an international referee. He is a member of the ITF demonstration team and is the director of the annual General Choi's Cup, an ITF tournament. He is also the founder and chairman of the Taekwon-do Instructor's Association and is the chairman of its board of examiners.

He resides in New Jersey, where he runs his own school, Suk Jun Kim's Taekwon-do.

THE SEQUENCES

Taekwon-do is noted for its kicking techniques, although it uses hands equally well. Taekwon-do has developed kicking methods to meet every situation. Demonstrated here are two advanced kicking techniques that serve a special purpose—surprise. These kicks work because they take the opponent by surprise, and the player will often score with them.

KICKING TECHNIQUES

The Twisting Kick

1. Start by facing your opponent (man on left in photo) (photo 14-1).

2. Your opponent attempts a lunge punch by sliding his front foot forward, and you pivot and twist, creating an angle that removes your opponent's target area, namely your head (photo 14-2).

3. With split-second timing, raise your leg (photo 14-3) and deliver a twisting kick to

your opponent's throat (photos 14-4 and 14-5). The beauty of the twisting kick is that, from the chamber position (see photo 14-3), there is no way to tell that it is a twisting kick until it is in motion, and then it is too late.

14-1

14-2

14-3

14-4

14-5

14-6

14-7

14-8

14-9

Axe Kick

1. Start by facing your opponent (man on left in photo) (photo 14-6).

2. Your opponent attempts a front roundhouse (turning) kick (photo 14-7). Twist your body at an angle that will evade the kicking action and jam the knee to prevent your opponent from extending the leg.

3. Counterattack by bringing your back foot into play through the execution of an axe kick to the opponent's face (photos 14-8 and 14-9).

CHAPTER 15
MICHELLE MAZZOCHETTI
A WOMAN'S VIEW OF FREE-FIGHTING

THE SEQUENCES

Mazzochetti demonstrates some of her most successful sport combinations. Like her training partner and coach Randy Pumputis (see Chapter 12), Mazzochetti believes in throwing combination after combination in the hope of scoring with one of the techniques. These combinations have been tested in the "ring" for efficiency.

Michelle Mazzochetti is one of the most successful female competitors on the East Coast today. A fighter of exceptional ability who has mastered a variety of kicking and punching combinations, she is one of the youngest legitimate female black belts in the country today.

Mazzochetti began her training under her cousin, the remarkable Debra Mazzochetti (see Chapter 21), but reached her competitive peak under the coaching of Randy Pumputis at the Pumputis Karate Academy in Greece, New York. She has appeared in such national publications as *Inside Karate* and *Official Karate*.

THE COMBINATIONS

Combination 1: Roundhouse Kick to Fake Back Kick Chamber to Setup Punch to Punch

In this combination Mazzochetti demonstrates the cleverness she is noted for in the ring.

Start by facing your opponent (woman on left in photo) in a ready stance (photo 15-1). Chamber your leg (photo 15-2) and throw a roundhouse kick at your opponent's head (photo 15-3). Return your leg to chamber position, showing your back (photo 15-4). This action will lead the opponent to think you are throwing a back kick, and the opponent will instinctively protect her midsection, leaving the head area open to attack.

Take advantage of this and throw a high punch to the attacker's face (photo 15-5), but throw it slowly enough for the opponent to block. This makes your opponent overconfident. You can then slam home a punch to your opponent's open midsection for a solid point (photo 15-6).

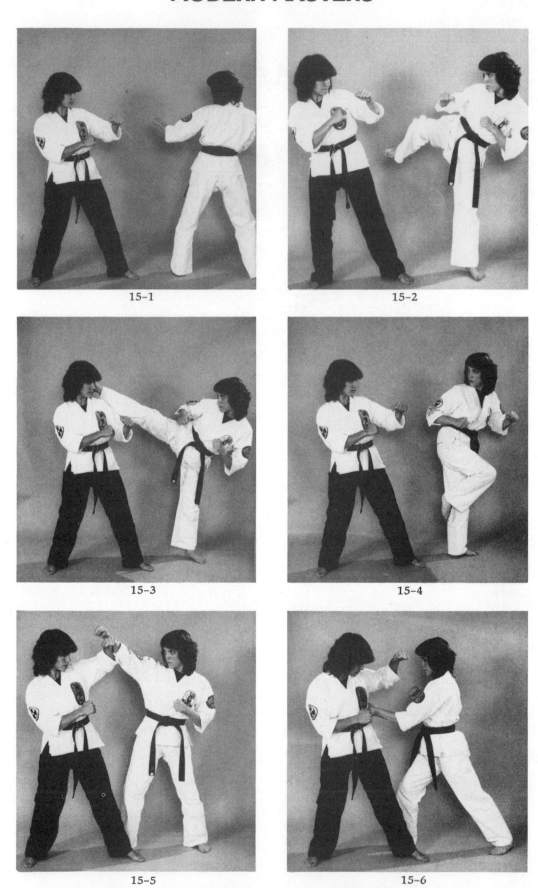

15-1

15-2

15-3

15-4

15-5

15-6

Combination 2: Setup Side Kick to Roundhouse Kick to Ridge Hand

Stand, facing your opponent (photo 15-7). Your opponent is a retreater in this case, meaning she constantly backs off, making it difficult for you to move in on her. To remedy this, throw a slow, short (of target area) side kick (photos 15-8 and 15-9), which your opponent steps back to avoid. However, seeing a chance, the opponent now charges in (photo 15-10) to strike. Simply throw another kick, this time a roundhouse, catching the opponent on the head (photo 15-11). While the opponent is still off guard, assure a point with a ridge hand to the face (photo 15-12).

15-7

15-8

15-9

15-10

15-11

15-12

Combination 3: Double Setup Punches to Point Punch

Stand, facing your opponent (photo 15-13). Throw a slow low punch, which your opponent blocks (photo 15-14). Next throw a mid-speed face punch, which your opponent blocks (photo 15-15). This move creates an opening at the opponent's midsection, which you take advantage of by throwing a reverse punch for the point (photo 15-16).

15-13

15-14

15-15

15-16

Combination 4: Side Kick to Roundhouse Kick

This is a favorite power combination of Mazzochetti's.

Begin it by facing your opponent in a stable ready stance (photo 15-17). Your opponent attempts to move in, but you stop her short with a side kick to the rib cage (photo 15-18). Finish the combination by rechambering your leg (photo 15-19) and throwing a roundhouse kick to your opponent's head (photo 15-20).

15-17

15-18

15-19

15-20

CHAPTER 16
DOUG IVAN
THROWING THE PERFECT KICK

Doug Ivan was born into martial arts, having trained in both Japan and the United States. His studies have included karate (Shito-ryu), judo, aikido, kendo, and *kobudo* (weapons). His weapons expertise includes mastery of nunchaku, sai, bo, tonfa, Phillipine *balisong* (butterfly knife), *katana* (Japanese sword), and various ninja weapons.

An avid actor, Doug Ivan has appeared in several major marital arts movies including *Enter the Ninja* and *The Karate Kid.* He has also appeared in non–martial arts movies. His most recent was the 1984 hit *Protocol.* His TV credits include commercials and the made-for-TV movie *The Last Ninja.*

Ivan is the chief instructor of the Newport/Costa Mesa school of the Japan Karate Federation (Orange County, California).

THE SEQUENCES

Ivan is a perfectionist when it comes to basic techniques. His philosophy is simple: True karate ability is achieved only after perfection of the basics.

Since karate kicking is of prime importance to today's youthful practitioners, Ivan gives his advice on and demonstration of two of karate's most important kicking techniques.

THE FRONT KICK

Basic Method

Assume a closed stance (heisoku-dachi) with both knees bent and arms extended at sides (photo 16-1). Chamber the kicking foot to the knee of the nonkicking leg (photo 16-2). Execute the kick, striking the target with the ball of the foot. Kick can be delivered to midsection (photo 16-3) or to face level (photo 16-4).

16-1

16-2

16-3

16-4

Important Points for Chamber Position

1. Raise the knee, keeping the sole of the foot parallel to the ground, but with the ball of the foot slightly higher than the heel.
2. Keep the shin almost perpendicular to the ground.
3. Pull back the heel as much as possible.
4. Curl the toes back (up) and tighten the ankle.
5. Relax the knee joint and keep it flexible.

Important Points in the Kicking Action

1. Flex the ankle and knee of the support leg.
2. Lean the upper body as much as possible in the direction of the kick. If you lean away from the kick, you will lose your balance. At worst, you will be propelled away from the target at the moment of impact.
3. Use the hips. Push them in the direction of the kick.

General Considerations

1. Always use the hips as well as the power of the legs.
2. Lock the kicking leg out fully and powerfully to prevent the reaction of the impact from pushing the leg back toward you.
3. When you use the ball of the foot as the striking weapon, tighten and strengthen the ankle so it can take the impact.

THE SIDE KICK

Basic Method

Assume a closed stance (heisoku-dachi), looking to your side (photo 16-5). Chamber the kicking foot to the knee of the support leg (photo 16-6) and deliver the side kick (photo 16-7).

16-5

16-6

16-7

Important Points for Chamber Position

1. Follow the same pointers as for the front kick.
2. Point the toes of the foot forward and direct the edge of the foot downward and parallel to the floor.

Important Points in Kicking Action

1. When kicking, strongly lock out the knee of the kicking leg as you rotate the hips and thrust out to the side, until the thigh and lower leg form one unbroken line. The sudden and complete locking out of the knee guarantees maximum power in the thrust kick.
2. The thrusting action of the kicking leg is strongest when your foot edge hits the target at a 90-degree angle.
3. Withdraw the kicking leg as nearly as possible along the same lines as you delivered it.

General Considerations

1. Avoid kicking the target with the toes or with the sole instead of the foot edge. Fully bend and tighten the ankle. Revolve your foot downward to the side and tighten it. As you kick, twist your foot inward as though you were trying to kick with the heel. By doing so, you will assure that all the surface along the edge of the foot will hit the target.
2. It is important to lock the knee of the kicking leg completely.

CHAPTER 17
JEAN DUTEAU
CLASSICAL CHINESE FREE-FIGHTING COMBINATIONS

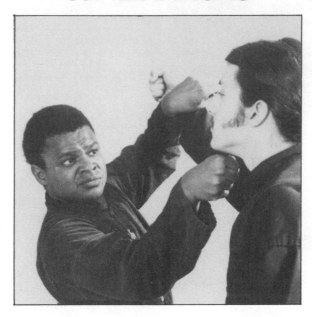

Jean Duteau began his study of kung-fu at an early age under the guidance of several instructors. Having an ambassador for a father, Jean studied several different martial arts in many different countries, including China and France (where he studied *savate,* French foot fighting).

Duteau's greatest understanding of kung-fu came under Alan Lee, a New York City–based Shaolin kung-fu instructor. Duteau has been featured in the *Official Karate Annual* (1984) and currently operates a *kwoon* (school) called Duteau's Shaolin Kung-fu Academy.

THE SEQUENCES

Duteau demonstrates classical free-fighting combinations that imitate the movements of animals and insects. Shaolin kung-fu, according to legend, was developed by watching various animals in combat. The monks at Shaolin patterned their body movements after these animals to develop a potent fighting art. The five main animals used were the dragon, tiger, leopard, snake, and crane.

THE COMBINATIONS

Combination 1

Face your opponent (man on left in photo) (photo 17-1). Your opponent attempts a straight punch. Block the punch (photo 17-2) and, trapping the opponent's punching hand (photos 17-3 and 17-4), counterstrike with a willow palm to the throat (photo 17-5). Finish the combination by reaching under the opponent's arm (photos 17-6 and 17-7), grasping his neck (photo 17-8), and twisting him to the ground (photos 17-9 and 17-10).

17-1

17-2

17-3

17-4

17-5

17-6

17-7

17-8

17-9

17-10

Combination 2

Stand, facing your opponent in a fighting stance (photo 17-11). Opponent attempts a punch, which you block with a willow palm block (photo 17-12). Opponent attempts to grab your blocking arm. Push his grasping attempt away with your other arm (photo 17-13), back-pivot, and deliver a double elbow strike (photos 17-14 and 17-15). Finish the combination by locking the opponent's arm (photo 17-16) and bringing him to the ground (photo 17-17).

17-11

17-12

17-13

17-14

17-15

17-16

17-17

Combination 3

Stand, facing your opponent in a stable ready posture (photo 17-18). Opponent attempts a punch, which you simultaneously block and counterstrike with a phoenix eye fist to the chest (photo 17-19). Trapping the opponent's punching hand (photo 17-20), sweep the opponent's lead leg forward (photo 17-21) and counterattack with a kick to the face (photos 17-22 and 17-23)

17-18

17-19

17-20

17-21

17-22

17-23

Combination 4

In this combination Duteau imitates the movements of the praying mantis.

Face your opponent (man on right in photo) (photo 17-24). Your opponent attempts a kick, which you block (photo 17-25) and trap (photo 17-26). Stepping deeply forward, counterstrike (photo 17-27) and push the opponent (photo 17-28) down to the ground (photos 17-29 and 17-30).

17-24

17-25

17-26

17-27

17-28

17-29

17-30

CHAPTER 18
DAN IVAN
FAVORITE FREE-FIGHTING TECHNIQUES

Dan Ivan is considered one of the pioneers of martial arts in America. He began his studies in Japan in 1948 and since that time has earned black belt ranks in two styles of karate and in judo, aikido, and kendo.

He is the founder of the Japan Karate Federation of America, which now has some 50 branches. In 1983, the International Martial Arts Federation, World Headquarters Japan, appointed him as director of the United States branch.

While stationed in Japan with the U.S. services, Ivan was with the Criminal Investigating Department (CID). As an investigator, he frequently worked undercover in the back alleys of Tokyo. He authored a book entitled *Tokyo Undercover* (Ohara), which chronicled his exploits in uncovering international crime. Ivan has been featured in every major martial arts publication: *Black Belt*, *Karate Illustrated*, *Official Karate*, and *Self-Defense World*.

Together with his son, Doug (see Chapter 16), Dan Ivan runs one of the most successful martial arts schools in the United States (in Costa Mesa, California).

THE SEQUENCES

Ivan demonstrates traditional karate techniques in free-fighting combinations that have been most successful for him.

TRADITIONAL KARATE FREE-FIGHTING TECHNIQUES

Blocking Drills

Ivan feels the key to good free-fighting ability lies in the ability to evade the opponent's attack. Evasion comes in many forms, but the most basic—and, for that matter, the most practical—is blocking.

In order to learn successful blocking skills, Ivan demonstrates the traditional practice of blocking drills. Found in many styles of Japanese karate, blocking drills involve one partner throwing technique after technique while the other partner simply attempts to block every attack.

It is best to begin blocking drills very slowly, building up in time to full power and full speed. Duration should start at one minute and build to five straight minutes.

Stand, facing your opponent (man on right in photo) (photo 18-1). Your opponent fixes his hip (photo 18-2) and delivers a reverse punch (photo 18-3), which you block by using a knife-hand inside-to-outside block (shuto-uchi-uke) (photo 18-4). Your opponent immediately follows with a second strike, which you again block (photos 18-5 and 18-6), using a similar technique. *Note: Ivan does not attempt a counterattack. Instead, he simply blocks each attack with solid blocking techniques in stable stances.*

18-1

18-2

18-3

18-4

18–5

18–6

Favorite Combination

Ivan's trademark is his ability to flow swiftly from one technique to another, utilizing his backgrounds in aikido and judo to take a man to the ground.

Face your opponent (man on right in photo) in a stable fighting posture (photo 18-7). As your opponent moves in for a lunge punch (photo 18-8), step to the side to evade the punch as you deliver a knife-hand block (photo 18-9). Grasping the opponent's punching hand (photo 18-10), chamber your leg

(photo 18-11) and deliver a roundhouse kick (photo 18-12) to the opponent's rib cage. Stepping down from the kick, follow through with an elbow strike to the head (photo 18-13). To finish the opponent, execute a judo throw (called ko-soto-gake), which involves hooking your foot around your opponent's ankle (photos 18-14 and 18-15) and throwing him to the ground (photos 18-16 and 18-17). Follow the throw with a stomp kick (fumi-komi) to the opponent's chest (photo 18-18).

18–7

18–8

18-9

18-10

18-11

18-12

18-13

18-14

18-15

18-16

18-17

18-18

PART IV
SELF-DEFENSE

The sequences demonstrated in Part IV are karate techniques used in self-defense situations against everyday attacks and in unusual situations such as against karate weapons (nunchaku and sai) or when your hands are tied.

Self-defense is a natural extension of karate techniques. Self-defense skill comes only after years of drilling the basic techniques and when the kata is understood and can be demonstrated with power and realism.

Each chapter offers something a little different. Some show how karate mixes with other arts (such as boxing or jujutsu), while others detail the use of karate by women. Whatever the situation, remember that true self-defense is avoiding a potential situation completely. Only when there is no other recourse should karate be relied upon.

CHAPTER 19
KICHIRO SHIMABUKU
TRADITIONAL ISSHIN-RYU KARATE AS SELF-DEFENSE

Kichiro Shimabuku is a tenth-degree black belt and current head of the Isshin-ryu (one-heart school) system of karate, founded by his father, Tatsuo Shimabuku, in 1954. Kichiro took on the role of Isshin-ryu grandmaster after the death of his father in 1975.

THE SEQUENCES

Karate training is the art of perfecting the basic techniques. Once these are mastered, the basics are applied in one of three ways: kata (see Part II), kumite (see Part III), or self-defense (Part IV).

Isshin-ryu karate is a mixture of Goju-ryu and Shorin-ryu techniques, along with some unique body movement methods and a punch that does not twist the fist, as in other forms of karate, but instead throws it straight out.

Master Shimabuku demonstrates some Isshin-ryu karate techniques in common self-defense situations as well as against martial arts weapons.

ISSHIN-RYU SELF-DEFENSE

Lapel Grab Defense

Opponent (man on left in photo) approaches you and grabs your lapels (photo 19-1). In response, you grab his sleeves (photo 19-2) and pull him forward into the force of your front kick (mae-geri) (photo 19-3). Stepping behind opponent, pull him over your leg (photos 19-4 and 19-5), smashing the attacker's back into the ground (photo 19-6). Finish the defense with a punch to the head (photo 19-7).

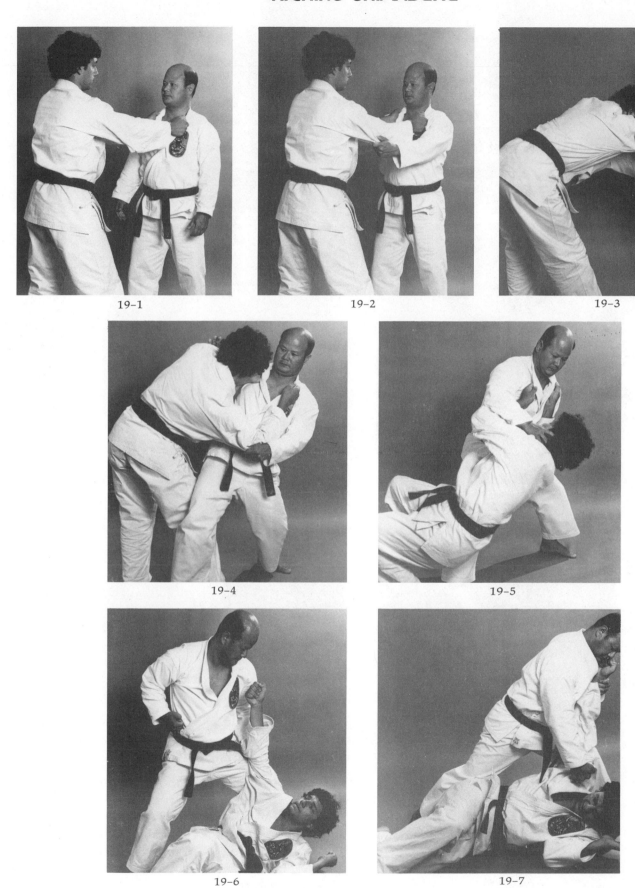

19-1

19-2

19-3

19-4

19-5

19-6

19-7

Punching Defense 1

Against a front punch (photo 19-8), guide the punch away from your face (photo 19-9) as you turn into the opponent in a clockwise arc (photo 19-10). When you are close enough, deliver a bone-crushing elbow strike (hiji-ate) to opponent's chest (photo 19-11).

19-8

19-9

19-10

19-11

Punching Defense 2

Face your opponent (photo 19-12). As opponent attempts a jab to your face (photo 19-13), grab the jabbing arm and pull it from its path (photo 19-14). Then step behind your opponent (photo 19-15), pull him off his feet (photo 19-16), and deliver a punch to attacker's head to finish him off (photos 19-17 and 19-18).

19–12

19–13

19–14

19–15

19–16

19–17

19–18

133

Club Defense

Against an overhead club attack (photo 19-19), block the attack with an X block (juji-uke) (photo 19-20), and carry the arm holding the club to your side to secure an arm lock (photo 19-21). Finish the attacker with a knee to the ribs (photo 19-22).

19–19

19–20

19–21

Nunchaku Defense

Stand facing an opponent, who is threatening you with a nunchaku (photo 19-23). As opponent attempts to hit you on the head, sidestep the attack (photo 19-24), making the weapon glide safely at your side. Finish the attacker with a lethal punch to his temple (photo 19-25).

19–22

19-23

19-24

19-25

Defense against Sai Attack

Opponent (man on right in photo) stands facing you with a pair of sai (traditional Okinawan fork weapon) (photo 19-26). As attacker stabs, sidestep the attack and grab the attacker's arm (photo 19-27). Finish the attacker with a cutting kick (fumi-kiri) to his knee (photo 19-28). Delivered with enough force, this kick can break the leg, ending the attack.

19-26

19-27

19-28

CHAPTER 20
MAS OYAMA
KYOKUSHINKAI-KAN KARATE AGAINST A GUN

Masutatsu Oyama (known worldwide as Mas Oyama) was born in 1923 in Korea. There at the age of nine, he studied kempo, jujutsu, and Shaolin kung-fu.

In 1937 he was sent to military school in Japan, and there he began studying Shotokan karate, training under Master Gichin Funakoshi for two years. After being drafted into the service, Oyama studied the Goju-ryu karate system at the Butokukai-kan under Neichu-so.

So devoted was he to martial arts that he traveled to Mt. Kiyosumi (Chiba Prefecture) and lived there for 18 months in seclusion, meditating and practicing the martial arts.

After returning to civilization, Oyama wanted to show the public the true meaning behind the martial arts and the power one can develop by living the *way*. He did this by fighting a bull *bare-handed* (the bull was marked for slaughter). He staggered it off its

feet with one punch and then, with a single knife-hand strike, removed its horn. He fought 52 bulls and never lost a match.

In 1956 Oyama founded the Kyokushinkai-kan system of karate, whose trademark is its Zen meditation, *tameshiwara* (breaking techniques), and full contact sparring (kumite).

THE SEQUENCES

Mas Oyama demonstrates two effective defenses against a gun. The techniques are from his book *What Is Karate* (Japan Publications, 1963) and are reprinted here by permission of Mas Oyama.

The first rule in defending against a gun is *not to defend!* Simply put, give the attacker what he wants, especially if it is just money. However, if the attacker is bent on taking not only your money, but also your life, you have nothing to lose by trying a solid defense.

20-1

20-2

20-3

20-4

GUN DEFENSES

Gun Defense 1

Opponent has placed his gun in your back and has told you to raise your hands (photo 20-1). Wiggle your left hand to draw opponent's attention to it. Then turn in the opposite direction, blocking the gun's way with the right hand (photo 20-2). Stepping behind the opponent with the left leg, trap the opponent's gun arm with your right arm and place your right hand on opponent's neck (photo 20-3). Applying backwards leverage, break the larnyx of the attacker (photo 20-4).

20–5

20–6

20–7

20–8

Gun Defense 2

Opponent has pointed his gun at your chest and tells you to raise your hands (photo 20-5). In a lightning-fast block, parry the gun out of the way with your right arm (photo 20-6). Securely grabbing the gun arm, kick the opponent's right leg with your left foot, breaking the attacker's leg at the knee joint (photo 20-7). Finish him off with a knife-hand strike (shuto-uchi) to attacker's larnyx (photo 20-8).

CHAPTER 21
DEBRA MAZZOCHETTI
SELF-DEFENSE FOR WOMEN

Debra Mazzochetti, an Isshin-ryu karate stylist, holds the rank of *yondan* (fourth-degree black belt) and is one of the highest-ranking females in America.

Having trained under Joe Jennings in the seventies, Mazzochetti went on to win the AAU Nationals in karate (fighting) and was featured prominently in the book *Winning Karate*, by Joe Jennings (Contemporary Books).

She teaches in Penfield, New York, where she runs one of the most successful martial arts schools in the country.

THE SEQUENCES

Karate is difficult for women because in order to be effective they must generate a good deal of power. It takes hard work and dedication, "especially for the female," says Mazzochetti.

"We [females] must work twice as hard to equal the natural strength of a man, so in order for a woman to be effective, she has to be willing to work for it. There are no magic formulas—except perhaps sweat and plenty of it."

When a woman is attacked she is usually grabbed and then pulled to the ground—in contrast to a man, who is usually punched. Therefore, Mazzochetti has chosen to demonstrate self-defense against body grabs that a woman is most likely to encounter.

BODY GRAB DEFENSE

Front Grab (Choke) Defense

An attacker grabs you around the neck (photo 21-1). Break the choke hold with a wedging block (kakiwake-uke) (photo 21-2) and immediately counter with a palm heel strike (teisho-uchi) to opponent's nose (photo 21-3). Grasping opponent's hair (photo 21-4), pull the opponent's face down onto your knee (photo 21-5), crushing his nose. Finish the defense with an arm lock (photo 21-6) and a knife-hand (shuto) strike to the back of the opponent's head (photo 21–7).

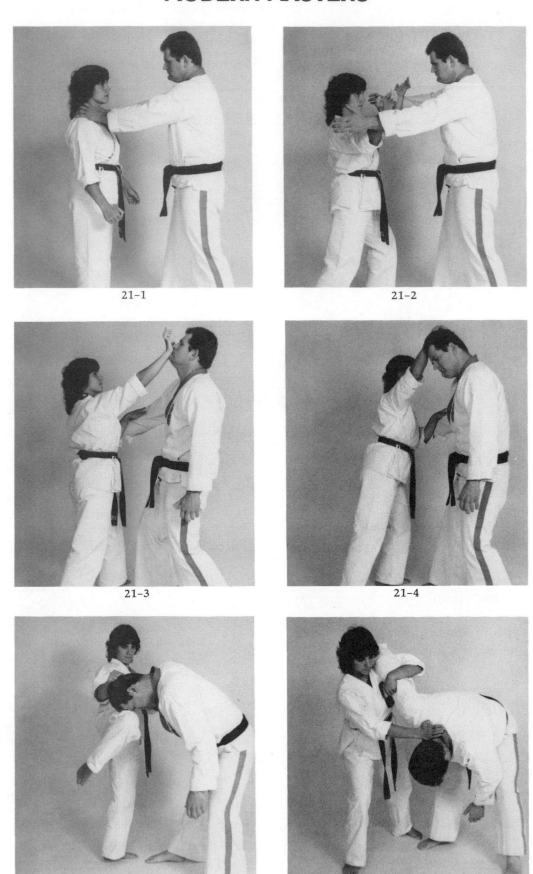

21-1

21-2

21-3

21-4

21-5

21-6

DEBRA MAZZOCHETTI

Arm Grab Defense

Opponent has seized your arm (photo 21-8). To stop opponent from taking you down, deliver a cutting kick (fumi-kiri) to opponent's knee and, without hesitation, use your arms and hip rotation to break the hold on your arm (photos 21-9, 21-10, and 21-11).

Going with the flow of your body movements, deliver a backhanded knife-hand (shuto) to opponent's nose (photo 21-12), grasp his head (photo 21-13), and, with a powerful twist, smash the opponent's head into the ground (photo 21-14).

21-7

21-8

21-9

21-10

21-11

21-12

21-13

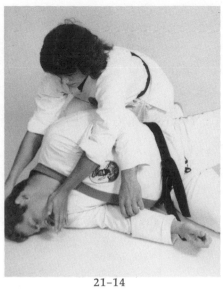

21-14

C H A P T E R 2 2
FUMIO DEMURA
SHITO-RYU KARATE AS SELF-DEFENSE

A former All-Japan karate champion, seventh-degree Itosu-kai (also known as Shito-ryu) karate black belt, Fumio Demura immigrated to the United States in 1965 at the request of his friend and partner, Dan Ivan.

Demura was elected to the "Black Belt Hall of Fame" (presented by *Black Belt* magazine) in 1969 as "Karate Instructor of the Year," and again in 1975 as the "Man of the Year." In 1973 he won the "Golden Fist Award" for "Outstanding Martial Artist of the Decade."

A student of Master Ryusho Sakagami (chairman of the Federation of All-Japan Karate-do Organizations) Demura also holds black belt ranks in kendo, kobudo, and judo. He is a seventh-degree karate black belt through IMAF (International Martial Arts Federation), and for this reason has been chosen to demonstrate this technique in the book.

He resides in Orange County, California, where he operates a chain of dojos with partner Dan Ivan.

THE SEQUENCES

Demura has a national reputation for clean technique that embodies power and realism. Although he is noted mainly for his skill with ancient Okinawan kobudo weapons, his self-defense demos of the early seventies were highly acclaimed.

In these sequences, Demura demonstrates his brand of realism and no nonsense in self-defense, using techniques from the Shito-ryu karate system.

SHITO-RYU DEFENSE

Defense against Arm Grab

As mentioned above, Demura is known for his technique, so pay close attention to the photos. In this demonstration Demura's technique is perfect.

You are confronted by an attacker (man on left in photos), who grabs your arm (photo

22-1

22-2

22-3

22-4

22-1). Pull your arm free by shifting your weight to the rear leg and yanking your arm free (photo 22-2). Shifting your weight forward into a back stance (ko-kutsu-dachi), execute a knife-hand strike (shuto-uchi) to opponent's nose (photo 22-3). Continuing to shift your weight forward (this time into a front stance), deliver a closepunch (ura-zuki) to opponent's midsection (photo 22-4).

22-5

22-6

22-7

22-8

Front Lapel Grab (or Choke) Defense

Note: This technique is also effective against a front choke.

The opponent grabs you by the lapels (photo 22-5). Raise both arms straight up in the air while bringing your body to an erect posture (photo 22-6). Slam your elbows down onto opponent's arms while you sink into a back stance (photo 22-7). This action will break the hold the opponent has on you. Moving into a front stance (zen-kutsu-dachi), execute a double thumb strike (morote yubi-uchi) to opponent's eyes (photo 22-8).

145

CHAPTER 23
PETER MANFREDI
MIXING BOXING AND KARATE FOR SELF-DEFENSE

Peter Manfredi is a second-degree black belt (nidan) in Shotokan karate under the Japan Karate Association and the All-Japan Seibukan Martial Arts and Ways Association. Manfredi runs his own karate club in Rochester, New York, called the Way of the Empty Hand.

In his early days of training, Manfredi began boxing and competed quite successfully, winning many amateur titles. Because of his background in boxing, Manfredi excelled in the hand-techniques of karate, developing unique combinations that combined the two arts. Manfredi took his blend of boxing and karate to the ring and won numerous karate titles. It is because of this that he was selected to demonstrate for this chapter.

THE SEQUENCES

Boxing has always been noted for its strong hand techniques and karate for its fabulous kicking maneuvers. Manfredi a second-degree black belt in Shotokan karate and an accomplished boxer, demonstrates his personal blend of these two arts in a survival situation.

KARATE-BOXING DEFENSE

Defense against a Punch

Face your opponent (man on left in photos) in a fighting stance (photo 23-1). Opponent attempts a punch to the head, which you block (photo 23-2). Follow through with a front kick to opponent's groin (not illustrated), a boxing right cross to opponent's head (photos 23-3 and 23-4), and a boxing uppercut to his ribs (photo 23-5). Finish the opponent off with a knife-hand strike (shuto-uchi) to the back of opponent's neck (photos 23-6 and 23-7).

23-1

23-2

23-3

23-4

23-5

23-6

23-7

Defense against a Front Choke

Face your opponent (photo 23-8). Opponent lunges at you and secures a tight hold around your neck (photo 23-9). Step back into a stable left front stance (zen-kutsu-dachi) (photo 23-10) and, using a wedging block (kakiwake-uke), break the grip around your neck (photo 23-11). Using your rear leg for momentum, swing your right leg back (photo 23-12) and bury a powerful knee kick (hizaga-shira-geri) in opponent's groin (photo 23-13). Using two lightning-fast boxing techniques, deliver an uppercut to opponent's chin (photos 23-14 and 23-15) and a right cross to the chin (photos 23-16 and 23-17). To finish off the downed opponent, deliver a bone-rattling stomping kick (fumi-komi) to attacker's groin (photos 23-18 and 23-19).

23-8

23-9

23-10

23-11

23-12

23-13

23-14

23-15

23-16

23-17

23-18

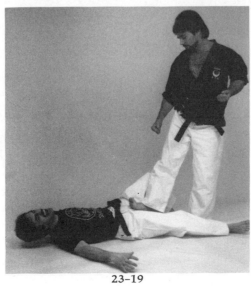

23-19

CHAPTER 24
FRANKIE "DR. SPEED" MITCHELL
SELF-DEFENSE IN SPECIAL SITUATIONS

Frankie "Dr. Speed" Mitchell holds black belt certification in Okinawan Goju-ryu karate and Shorin-ryu karate. He is currently certified as a *godan* (fifth-degree black belt) from Aaron Banks of New York City (himself a tenth dan).

Mitchell with his uncle Richard Brooks formulated the *Hatha-goju-ryu* style of karate—a style that emphasizes yoga discipline and philosophy in its training. In addition, the Hatha-goju style combines a number of defenses against unusual situations, such as being attacked with an axe, being attacked with hands tied, etc. Since they are not found in many other systems, we have elected Frankie to illustrate some of these.

THE SEQUENCES

Every so often a karateka finds himself trapped in a special situation; that is, a situation in which only the most skilled of martial artists would survive. Being pinned to the floor, being attacked with an axe, or being attacked with a knife when your hands are tied are examples. These are the special situations that Frankie Mitchell, a Hatha-goju-ryu black belt, addresses in the following photos.

SPECIAL-SITUATION DEFENSE

Floor Pin Defense

You have been pinned to the floor and are being choked (photo 24-1). Placing your palm on the elbow of your attacker's arm (photo 24-2), hyperextend your opponent's elbow, breaking the grip from around your throat (photo 24-3). Roll your opponent onto his back (photo 24-4) and come to a position directly over him. Finish him off with a chest-shattering elbow strike (hiji-ate) (photo 24-5).

24-1

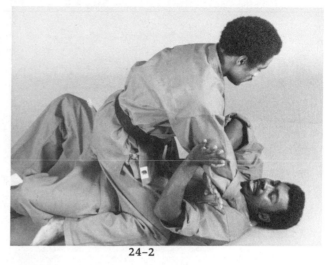

24-2

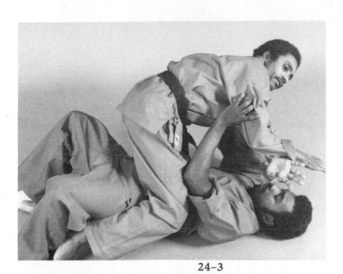

24-3

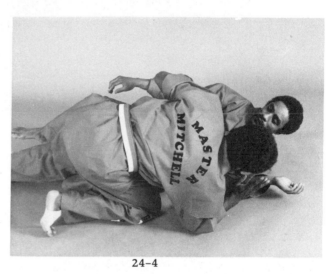

24-4

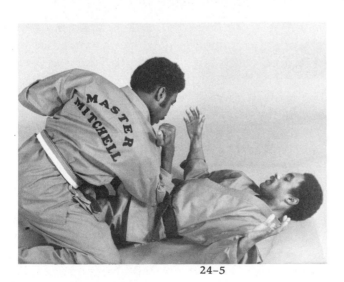

24-5

Seated Defense

You are attacked from behind as you sit on a chair (photo 24-6). The opponent has secured a choke hold. Grasp your opponent's arm and pull straight down to relieve the pressure on your windpipe (photo 24-7). To subdue the opponent, deliver a backfist strike (uraken-uchi) to the bone under the opponent's eye (photo 24-8). Delivered with enough power, this technique will break the opponent's cheekbone.

To finish the opponent off, reach up and grasp the opponent by the collar (photo 24-9) and, standing up, secure an arm lock on your attacker's arm (photo 24-10). Pressure, with this arm lock, is applied against the shoulder by pulling straight down on the wrist.

24-6

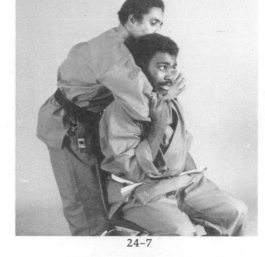

24-7

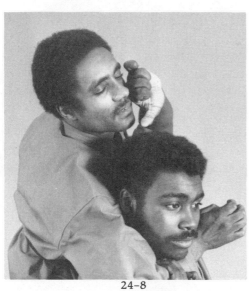

24-8

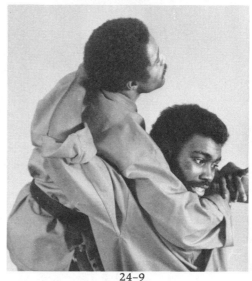

24-9

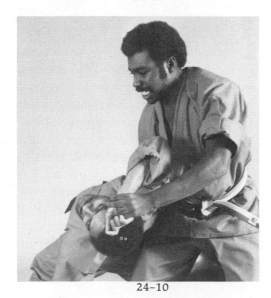

24-10

Defense against Knife when Hands Are Tied

Face your opponent with your hands tied in front of you (photo 24-11). To your surprise your attacker is carrying a knife. Seeing the knife slash coming at your face (photo 24-12), extend your arms and block the attack (photo 24-13). Your next moves must be lightning fast and accurate since you will not be given a second chance. Immediately drop to the ground to avoid another slash (photo 24-14) and deliver a crippling roundhouse kick (ma-washi-geri) to opponent's groin (photo 24-15).

24–11

24–12

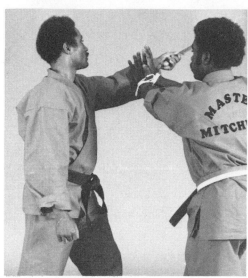

24–13

24–14

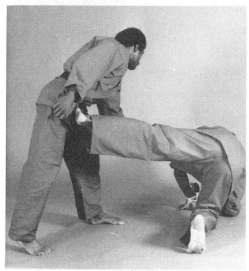

24–15

Defense against an Axe

Face your opponent who is holding an axe over your head (photo 24-16). Attacker attempts a downward blow to your skull, but you sidestep the action and block the attack with a knife-hand block (shuto-uke) (photo 24-17). Stepping to the side of your opponent, swing your arm up overhead (photo 24-18), wrapping it around the attacker's arm (photo 24-19), preventing him from using the axe again. Finish the attack by hyperextending the attacker's elbow, breaking his arm (photo 24-20).

24-16

24-17

24-18

24-19

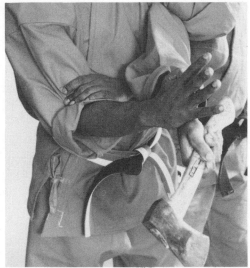

24-20

CHAPTER 25
GEORGE R. PARULSKI, JR.
MIXING KARATE AND JUJUTSU

Parulski holds a fourth-degree black belt in karate (yondan) under the direction of the Japan Karate Association, All-Japan Seibukan Martial Arts and Ways Association, and the International Martial Arts Federation.

There are very few individuals who have competed successfully in both karate and judo. Parulski has won national titles in each art—an accomplishment rivaled by only a few others. Because of his skill in aiki-jujutsu, an art that specializes in close-in fighting techniques, Parulski's personal self-defense skills blend both arts creating a unique and effective system. Parulski demonstrates this mixture in a few impressive sequences.

THE SEQUENCES

Many have said time and again that the best method of self-defense is a mixture of karate and jujutsu/judo techniques. The reason is that karate, with its strikes and kicks, is a long-range method of fighting, and jujutsu, with its throws and locks, is a short-range

combat system. The two complement each other.

Parulski has achieved high ranks in karate and Tenshin-shin'yo-ryu aiki-jujutsu (with training in Kito-ryu jujutsu, as well). In the following sequences he mixes karate and jujutsu to defend himself against weapon attacks.

KARATE-JUJUTSU DEFENSE

Defense against a Club

Stand, facing your opponent (man on right in photo), who is intent on smashing your skull with a club (photo 25-1). As the attacker swings the weapon, backstep to get out of the way of the attack, chamber your foot for a kick, and stop the weapon with a knife-hand block (photo 25-2). With the hand that blocked the weapon, grab the attacker's arm to prevent him from swinging at you again and bury a side kick (photo 25-3) deep in the attacker's chest. As you place your kicking foot down, follow through with a frontal

25-1

25-2

25-3

25-4

25-5

elbow attack (mae-empi-uchi) to opponent's face (photo 25-4). Using a jujutsu technique, place your arm under the opponent's arm (with the weapon) and pull down sharply on opponent's arm, dislocating the shoulder joint (photo 25-5). Then reach up, grab the opponent's neck, and pull sharply on the attacker's head as you throw your body weight forward (photo 25-6). This movement throws the attacker to the ground (photo 25-7) in a somersault action. Staying close to the opponent's side to control the weapon hand, finish the defense with a punch to opponent's face (photo 25-8)

25-6   25-7   25-8

Knife Defense

Stand, facing your opponent, who holds his weapon close to his forearm (photo 25-9). As the attacker tries to slash, backstep to avoid getting your face cut and begin to guide the attacker's arm (photo 25-10) in the direction of the arc created by the attacker's own force of attack (photo 25-11). Continuing to guide the knife, initiate your own force, burying the knife in the attacker's chest (photo 25-12). Then apply an arm lock (photo 25-13), dislocating the opponent's shoulder (photo 25-14), deliver a knee kick to opponent's face (photo 25-15), and pull the weapon free as opponent falls to the floor (photos 25-16 and 25-17).

25-9   25-10

25-11

25-12

25-13

25-14

25-15

25–16

25–17

PART V

WEAPONS

When empty-hand karate was born on Okinawa (see Chapter 1), the Okinawans also applied their knowledge and skills to the commonplace—their farm tools. *Kobudo* (the art of using Okinawan farm tools as weapons) developed from this. (It should be noted that the weapons arts were first known as *ti-gua*. *Kobudo* is a term coined during the late nineteenth century.)

The *bo* (staff) and the *eku* (oar) have common ancestry, coming from fishing villages. By tying a knife to the tip of the bo, which was used to push their boats upstream, the staff was transformed into a lance.

The *tonfa* was originally a handle for a millstone (the grip was originally much longer and had to be adapted to self-defense purposes), which the farmers converted into twirling weapons. Looking like two pieces of wood with small off-centered handles, the tonfa appears innocent enough, but in the hands of a knowledgeable farmer, it became a defense against *ronin* (outlaw samurai).

The *nunchaku* is the ultimate in simplicity, being two foot-long sticks tied together by a piece of rope or chain. It could be a garrote, a club, or a swinging weapon (traveling at speeds up to 150 miles an hour).

The *sai* and the *nunte* also have common history, although some believe the nunte preceded the sai by many years. Both appear the same at a glance, but the sai has a handle, while the nunte has a point. The sai has a double guard pointing away from the handle; the nunte has a double guard pointing in opposite directions.

Although the study of karate has diverse facets, modern-day karate is primarily considered self-defense without weapons. It is only at the advanced ranks that the art of kobudo comes into play, and in many karate systems kobudo never enters into training.

Kobudo training is useful because:

1. Kobudo plays an important historical role in karate and should be preserved for its cultural significance.
2. Weapons training can develop dexterity that could not be otherwise achieved through normal training. With practice, karate weapons become an extension of your body.

161

3. Kobudo develops fluid movement. Reactions flow from one step to another, a plus for free-fighting.

4. Karate weapons require physical and mental balance and coordination, skills that improve free-fighting ability as well as empty-hand kata ability (see Part II).

5. Some karate weapons are still practical as methods of self-defense. Weapons like the nunchaku can be concealed on your person and used for self-defense. (*Check local laws before you carry any weapon to be sure you have the legal right to use that particular weapon.*)

Whatever the reason for your interest in kobudo, be it tool or weapon, it has proven to be an interesting and useful link with the past as well as a method of study that continues to help karateka mature.

CHAPTER 26
RICHARD BROOKS
ANCIENT OKINAWAN WEAPONS

Richard Brooks began his study of karate in the service while stationed overseas. Brooks, a fourth-degree black belt in Shorin-ryu karate, believes in learning as much as possible about *all* martial arts in order to grow fully as a human being.

Shorin-ryu karate is noted for its techniques with weapons (weapons make up a quarter of the system). Where other styles of karate treat weapons training as an extra, Shorin-ryu looks at weapons as an essential ingredient to the full development of the martial artist. It is for this reason that Brooks was selected to appear in this section.

An educator by trade, he teaches in Syracuse, New York, and is a master of weapons.

THE SEQUENCES

Brooks demonstrates sequences using sev-eral different Okinawan Kobudo weapons—Kama, sai, nunchaku, and short sticks—against a staff.

KOBUDO SEQUENCES

The Kama (Sickle)

1. Stand, facing your opponent (man on right in photo), who is armed with a bo (staff). You are armed with the kama (photo 26-1).

2. Opponent attempts to strike you on the head. Sidestep the attack and sweep the weapon aside with the kama (photo 26-2).

3. Bringing the staff to your side (for safety and control), backstep (photo 26-3), spin counterclockwise, and deliver a rear slash at opponent's head (photo 26-4) and an upward slash to the groin (photo 26-5).

26-1

26-2

26-3

26-4

26-5

The Sai (Fork)

1. In a fighting stance, face your opponent who is armed with a bo (photo 26-6).

2. Opponent attempts to strike you on the top of the head. Step forward and block the attack by crossing the shafts of the weapons and blocking the bo with the middle of the X (photo 26-7).

3. Counterattack by poking at the opponent's eyes (photos 26-8 and 26-9) and striking the opponent in the throat with the butt of the sai's handle (photo 26-10).

26-6

26-7

26-8

26-9

26-10

The Nunchaku

1. Stand, facing your opponent (man on left in photo), who is armed with a bo (photo 26-11).

2. The opponent steps back to prepare a thrusting action. Raise your weapon to ready yourself (photo 26-12).

3. As the opponent thrusts, sidestep the attack and guide the bo away with the nunchaku (photo 26-13).

4. Counterattack by thrusting the ends of the nunchaku into the opponent's throat (photo 26-14).

26-11

26-12

26-13

26-14

26-15

Short Sticks

1. Face your opponent (man on right in photo) armed with short sticks. Your opponent is armed with a bo (photo 26-15).

2. Opponent attempts to thrust the bo into your eyes. Stop the attack by pushing the staff away with the medium stick (photo 26-16).

3. Counterattack with three lightning-fast techniques: a thrust to the groin (photo 26-17), a strike to the inside of the knee joint (photo 26-18), and a strike to the back of the head (photo 26-19).

26–16

26–17

26–18

26–19

CHAPTER 27
RON DUNCAN
MODERN-DAY NINJA DEMONSTRATES USE OF SHORT STICK

Ronald Duncan is a weapons expert and modern-day ninja. Duncan is considered a pioneer of martial arts on the East Coast (see Chapter 2), having opened a karate school in 1956. He is noted for his exciting seminars and demonstrations, where he always displays his expert weapons ability.

Duncan holds black belt degrees in karate, jujutsu, and judo and operates a martial arts school in New York City.

THE SEQUENCES

Duncan demonstrates the use of the short stick to defend himself against an opponent who is threatening him with a knife. The techniques are clean and realistic.

SHORT STICK

Defense 1

1. Opponent (man on left in photo) threatens you with a knife and attempts a stab at your face.

2. Block the stabbing action with your short stick using your free hand to support the weapon (photo 27-1).

3. With your free hand, grasp the wrist of the hand holding the weapon (photo 27-2) and sharply strike the forearm nerve center (about one or two inches below elbow) (photo 27-3), forcing opponent to drop his weapon (photo 27-4).

27-1

27-2

27-3

27-4

Defense 2

1. You are contfronted by an opponent who is carrying a knife.

2. Opponent attempts a low cut to your legs. Stop the attack by striking the opponent's wrist with your short stick (photo 27-

5). The force of the strike makes the opponent drop his weapon.

3. Counterattack with three lightning-fast techniques: a stab to the side of the head (photo 27-6), a stab to the eyes (photo 27-7), and a downward strike to the nose (photo 27-8).

27-5

27-6

27-7

27-8

27-9

Defense 3

1. You are facing a crazed knife-carrying opponent, who is about to stab you with a downward action (photo 27-9).

2. Sidestep out of the way of the attack and simultaneously strike the opponent on the wrist with your short stick, forcing him to release the weapon (photo 27-10).

3. Moving quickly behind the opponent (photo 27-11), deliver an extremely powerful blow to the back of opponent's neck (photo 27-12).

Note: Delivered with enough power, a blow to the back of the neck causes unconsciousness, forcing the opponent to fall to the ground (photo 27-13).

27–10

27–11

27–12

27–13

Defense 4

1. Stand, facing your opponent, who is carrying a knife.

2. The opponent attempts to backhand slash you across the face. Stop the attack with your short stick (photo 27-14).

3. To secure the weapon, grasp the attacker's wrist and counterattack with a powerful strike to the back of the head (photo 27-15) and a follow-up jab to the face (photo 27-16).

4. Securing the attacker's neck in a lock (photo 27-17), roll the attacker over (photo 27-18) onto the ground and deliver a follow-up strike to the groin (photo 27-19).

5. Finish the defense by stabbing the attacker in the throat (photo 27-20).

27–14

27-15

27-16

27-17

27-18

27-19

27-20

INDEX

Adventures of Ozzie and Harriet,
    10
aiki-jujutsu, 14, 155
All-American Karate Federation, 12
All-Japan Seibukan Martial Arts
    and Ways Association, 6, 146,
    155
Arabia, 5
Avengers, The, 10
axe kick, 108

balisong knife, 114
Banks, Aaron, 12–13, 150
Bein Hasan, 3
Big Boss, The, 11
Billy Jack, 10
Biographies of the High Priests, 4
Black Belt Magazine, 124, 143
blocking drills, 124
bo, 161
Bodhidharma, 4, 5
boxing, 146
Breaker, Breaker, 69
Brooks, Richard, 163–167
bunkai, 18
Butokukai-kan, 136

Casel, Tayari, 100
Central Pacific Railroad, 7
certification, 16

Ch'an, *see* Zen
ch'ang-ch'uan, 100
China Town Dojo, 12
Chinese Connection, The, 11
ching-ling, 4
Chou Dynasty, 4
Chow, William, 8
ch'uan-fa, 4
CNY Dojo, 14
Combat Karate, 12
coolies, 7

daimyo, 5
Demura, Fumio, 12, 143–145
Detectives, The, 10
Dharuma, 4
Dharuma Taishi, 4
dojo, 6
double kicks, 91–93
Dunbar Center, 19
Duncan Ronald, 12, 168–174
Duteau, Jean, 118–123

East Coast Demo Team, 19
Edo, 5
Edwards, Blake, 9–10
Egypt, 3
eku, 161
Emperado, Ardiano, 8
Enter the Dragon, 11, 14

Enter the Ninja, 114
ESPN, 16
Eye for an Eye, 69

Fists of Fury, 11
Five Fingers of Death, 10
Force of One, 69
Forced Vengeance, 69
Fox, Ed, 100–105
free-fighting, 67
front kick, 114–116
Funakoshi, Gichin, 6, 31

gi, 46
Goju-ryu, 6, 7, 80
Gojushiho-kata, 19–30
"Golden Fists Awards," 143
Good Guys Wear Black, 69
Green Hornet, The, 10
goshin-do, 58
ground fighting, 100–105

haito-uchi, 89
Hashi, King, 5
Hatchet Men, *see* Tongs
Hatha Goju-ryu, 19, 150
Hawaii, 7
Heian kata, 31
himitsu, 18, 58

KARATE'S
MODERN MASTERS

Honan, 4
Honey West, 10

Iliad, 3
Inside Karate Magazine, 109
International Martial Arts
  Federation, 12, 124, 143, 165
ippon kumite, 67, 80
Isshin-ryu Karate, 11, 130
Itosu-kai, 143
Ivan, Dan, 12, 124–128
Ivan, Doug, 114–117, 124

Japan Karate Association, 6, 12,
  155
Java, 5
Jennings, Joe, 139
jiaolia, 4
jiyu kumite, 67
judo, 8
jujutsu, 136, 155

kajukenbo, 8
kama, 163–164
Kanku-dai kata, 31–46
Kanku-sho kata, 47–57
kata, 17–18
kata competition tips, 46
karate, 5
Karate for the Masses, 87
Karate Illustrated Magazine, 94, 124
karate-jutsu, 6
Karate Kid, The, 16, 114
Karate Power, 19
kempo, 7, 58, 136
kenpo, 8
Khashatriya, 3, 4
kickboxing, 87
kicking tips, 75–79
Kim, Suk Jun, 106–108
kisami-zuki, 87–88
kobudo, 161
Korea, 5
Kuhl, John, 12
kumite, *see* free- fighting
kung-fu, 4, 7, 100
"Kung-fu" (Televison Show), 10, 14
Kung Syang, 5
kupiganagumi, 100
Kusanku, 5, 31
kwoon, 118
kyokushinkai-kan, 6, 136

Lane, Frank, 14, 31
Last Ninja, 114
Lee, Alan, 118
Lee, Bruce, 10, 11
Lee Strasberg School of Acting, 69

Lewis, Joe, 87–90
Liang Dynasty, 4
lo-han, 5
Lowe, Ed, 8

Malacca, 5
Manfredi, Peter, 47–57, 146–149
Mattson, George, 11–12
Mazzochetti, Debra, 109, 139–142
Mazzochetti, Michelle, 109–113
McCarthy, Mark, 91–93
Merriman, Chuck, 12
Mesopotamia, 3
Mitchell, Frankie, 19–30, 150–154
Milton, 3
Mitose, James, 7, 8
Miyagi, Chojun, 6, 7
Musacchio, Peter, 80–86

Nagle, Don, 11
Naha-te, 6
Nanking, 4
neichia, 5
ninja, 168
Nishiyama, Hidetaka, 12
Norris, Chuck, 14–15, 69–74
Northern Dynasty, 14
nunchaku, 161, 165
nunte, 161
Nuuana YMCA, 7

Ochiai, Hidy, 100
Octagon, The, 69
Official Karate Magazine, x, xiii, 109,
  118
Okinawa, 5
Olympics (early), 3
Orbillo, Joe, 87
Oshima, Tsutomu, 9, 12
Oyama, Mas, 136–138

pancratium, 3
Patterson, Cecil, 11
Parker, Ed, 8, 9, 10
Parulski, George, 31–46, 155–159
Pearl Harbor, 6
Peichin Takahara, 6
Pink Panther, The, 10
Presley, Elvis, 9
Protocol, 114
Prajnatara, 4
Pumputis, Randy, 94–99, 109

Records of the Transmission of the Lamp,
  4
reishiki, 6
renshi, 80

Return of the Dragon, 11, 69
ronin, 161

sai, 161, 164
saifa kata, 58, 59–65
Saigo, 14
Satsuma, 5
savate, 118
self-defense, 129
Self-Defense World Magazine, 124
Shaolin, 4
Shao-shih, Mt., 5
Shang Dynasty, 4
Shimabuku, Eizu, 87
Shimabuku, Kichiro, 130–135
Shimabuku, Tatsuo, 11, 58, 130
Shimatsu, 5
Shito-ryu, 6
Shobukan Goju-ryu karate, 80
shogun, 5
"Shogun" (Television Show), 16
Shot in the Dark, 10
shotokan, 6
Shorin-ryu, 6, 58
short sticks, 166–167, 169–172
Shuri-te, 6, 7
Siamese fighting, 5
Silent Rage, 69
Sinew Change Classic, 5
Sofuku Matsumura, 6
Soken Matsumura, 6
Southern Dynasty, 4
Special Situation Self-defense,
  150–154
Spinning Cobras, 19
sport combinations, 94–99
su-bak, 5
Suganda, King, 4
Sumatra, 5
Sung Mountains, 5

Taekwon-do, 91
Takagi, Kichinosuku, 6, 14
tameshiwara, 136
Tamo, 4
T'ang Dynasty, 6
tang-so-do, 69
te, 6
Tea, History of, 5
Tegner, Bruce, 9–10
Theogenes, 3
tode, 5, 6
Tde Sakugawa, 5
tongs, 7
Tokugawa, Ieyasu, 5
tonfa, 161
Traceys, 14–15
Trias, Robert, 8
twisting kick, 106–107

INDEX

Uechi-ryu karate, 12
United States Karate Association, 8
ura-zuki, 88–89
Urban, Peter, 12, 14

vajramushti, 4
Van Clief, Ron, 12
Van Lenten, Frank, 58–62

waichia, 5
Wado-ryu, 6, 11
Wallace, Bill, 75–79
Washing Marrow Classic, 5
Way of Karate, 11
weapons, 161–162
What is Karate, 136
Wild, Wild West, The, 10
Winning Karate, 139
Wrecking Crew, 69

Wu, Emperor, 4

Yabi, Kentsu, 7
Yamaguchi, Gogen, 12
Yamaguchi, Gosei, 14
yoga, 150
Young, 8
Yuang-tsu River, 4
Zen, 4, 5